MW01127438

Reviving The
AMERICAN
DREAM

in Southern California

HOW TO PURCHASE A HOME & PAY IT OFF IN 5 YEARS

LLOYD MIZE

Reviving The American Dream In Southern California,

How To Purchase a Home & Pay it Off in 5 Years

Published by

REAL ESTATE SYSTEM
Purchase a Home & Pay It Off in 5 Years!

Copyright © 2013 by Lloyd Mize

ISBN: 978-1-937506-33-9

Printed in the United States of America

ACKNOWLEDGEMENTS

Thank you to Renee, my wife and soul mate for twenty-six years and to the other ladies in my life my mom Nita, Pagie my mother-in-law and my sister Marilyn Gwen. I have much appreciation and gratitude for my extended family and community. My extended professional business network, the members of Wine Country Business Growers BNI® located in Temecula California, Twin Cities Toastmasters and fellow Toastmaster members who continue to build into my life and me into theirs. My Real Estate team, Pacific Coast Realty Group Inc. James Brennan, Susan Aiken and agents, DP Property Management, Catherine Perrotta, Amanda and agents, my core team, Harvest Team Inc. Kathy Parks and a special thank you to our team manager and chief administrator, Felipe Flores. Southwest Riverside California Association of Realtors® is my Southern California local board of Realtors® and base network of Realtor® professionals. Tyler Woodward, thank you for being my chief book administrator and producer. I am a third generation real estate broker. My father Jimmie Mize pulled me into the fantastic business of real estate: In 1978, thanks Dad. Dawn Sneed, CEO of Olive Brand and Jonnie Fox of The Magnolia School of Etiquette and Protocol for your wonderful and timely assistance with the "2nd edition" and editing. Finally my gratitude for my Lord and God, Jesus Christ thank you for my faith and all you have blessed me with.

As an accomplished Southern California Realtor®, trainer, speaker and writer I can speak to the practices and strategies Lloyd gives in his book, they work. Lloyd speaks and writes from experiences. I recommend his book to clients looking to buy and sell real estate and Realtors®. It's a timely and great message.

— Marcus Slaton,
Mentor, Cobalt Real Estate Santa Clarita,
Author, "Motivate to Tri"

What does health and wellness have to do with real estate? As a Certified Master Fitness Trainer, I am always interested how different careers choose to view the health and wellness component of their life. Sure an expert can walk the walk in their area of expertise but do they talk the talk and walk the walk in all aspects of their life? Lloyd absolutely does and throughout Chapter 6 he imparts a great overview of how you can make small changes that will help you become a better and healthier person. The simple, easy to implement and most importantly realistic changes he suggest will send you on your way to having and owning what you want for your life."

— Bobby Kelly, www.ResultsOnly.com,
President of Results Only,
Author of "Body Solution"

CONTENTS

Introduction 7

Chapter 1: How to Purchase Your Home 17

Chapter 2: Know Exactly What You Want Out of a Home 35

Chapter 3: Why Own and What to Know 45

Chapter 4: Making More Money 53

Chapter 5: Reinventing Yourself 79

Chapter 6: Health and Wellness in Real Estate 101

Chapter 7: Purchasing Investment Property 111

Chapter 8: Really, Purchase a
            Home and Pay it off in Five Years? 123

Chapter 9: Go to Guide, Links,
            References and Networks 131

INTRODUCTION

Acquisition of property is the most common way that people realize the "American Dream." Since the discovery of the New World, people have flocked to our country, driven by hopes of creating a better quality of life for themselves and their family. Historically, real estate is the straightest, fastest road to building sustainable wealth.

Property ownership, meaning property that is owned free and clear with no mortgage or debt, provides financial comfort, freedom and power in your life. Owning property puts you in a position to make better choices. It allows you to take advantage of wonderful opportunities that other people don't even know exist. Though this is all common knowledge, free and clear/debt free property ownership remains an unexplored possibility for most.

Southern California holds fantastic opportunities for home ownership and other types of real estate investments. Your task is to recognize the opportunities, and position yourself to be the right person at the right time. Let me give you an example of what I'm talking about from my own experience.

In 1984, the real estate market in Southern California was depressed. In fact, at that year's California Association of Realtors Conference in San Francisco, a representative from a very large national bank said, "You real estate agents might as well take the next couple of years off." Interest rates were through the roof, which certainly didn't help matters. I was a 27-year-old, broke real estate agent. My own poor planning had consumed my cash. My credit was not good. My lack of steady income, combined with my less than favorable credit, meant I did not own a home or any other real estate investments. I was frustrated! After all, real estate was my business, and I did not have any to call my own.

There was a beach community in Port Hueneme located in Ventura County that hosts a condominium association known as Surfside III. At the time, beautiful beachfront listings were available for about $80,000 for a one bedroom, one bathroom unit, to $120,000 for a 2 bedroom 2 bath unit. The balconies in the complex were small. Almost all of the units were situated with beautiful Southern California beach and ocean views.

The one exception was a particular one bedroom, one bath condominium that had remained on the market much longer than the other units. I developed an interest in this property. My real estate gears engaged, and I became intrigued. I could see the potential with this one bedroom unit. All the other real estate agents—and potential buyers—showed no interest.

The potential was there, even if no one else saw it. My plan was to offer a lower, but reasonable, purchase price and hold the unit for twelve to twenty-four months. That would allow this condo to catch up with the values of the rest of the units in the complex. With just a 5% down payment, the fair market rent would cover the monthly payments. To unlock the unit's "unseen potential" I wanted to create a "model" look and feel to the condo. I wanted to give it energy, so that it would be attractive and desirable to potential buyers when I eventually resold the unit.

I had a plan. What I didn't have was an income I could document, a down payment, and good credit. All these things kept me from qualifying for a loan or mortgage to purchase the condo. I needed a partner!

A good friend had done well for himself since high school. He had a fantastic job, spotless credit, seemed to always have extra cash, and loved a great deal. I called him and we talked about the beachfront condo, and the profit potential it held. He listened to my observations and plans for the unit. We debated whether it really was a great deal. I'm not sure if it was because of our friendship, or because he saw the same potential I did, but we agreed on our strategy and were on our way.

He fronted the 5% down payment, and supplied the good credit and documented income. He also maintained a wonderful attitude. Do not overlook the importance of a positive attitude when looking for a business partner. It may seem like a small thing, but I have found it can make a world of difference in terms of your success.

We offered approximately $10,000 less than the list price—the seller agreed. We had purchased our first investment property! From the beginning, I set out to create value for the property, the "model like look and feel." If you walked about on the miniature balcony of my little project and craned your neck about 180 degrees, you could just catch a glimpse of the beach and ocean before you had to call your chiropractor to straighten out your neck and back. On the wall opposite this strained view there was a large, blank space where an awesome piece of art or a big screen television could have easily rested.

But, I had another plan for this section of the condo. I covered almost the entire wall with an enormous mirror. Now, that beautiful beach and ocean view reflected directly into the living room. This allowed us to create a rental ad that read: "A beautiful beachfront view right inside your living room." We immediately rented the unit! In just two years, the property appreciated, just as we had anticipated. We made approximately $40,000 in profit! Selling the condo gave me the resources and position I needed to make my next move.

The point of this story is not to brag on myself. The point is simply this: You can accomplish great things if you position yourself as the right person for the right opportunities. Avoid making the assumption that certain opportunities are not for you. Don't buy into the myth that good opportunities are a matter of luck, or only knock on the doors of lucky people. With no money or credit, would anyone have thought I would be the right person to buy that condominium? Most people did not consider that condo the right property to buy. What I did have was the experience and creativity to develop a solution where none was obvious to most.

In this book, I am going to show you that YOU are the right person to purchase property, and pay it off sooner than later. It's a simple matter of developing a vision of what you want, believing that you are ready, and moving to create the next steps for yourself—an action plan. You are the right person! You just have to educate yourself to understand the value of what you have, know what to look for, and realize the potential of what you can accomplish. Opportunities are abound for everyone, no matter your current position in life. You just need to be ready to see them and receive them.

In 1984, we purchased that little condominium. In 1986, we sold it for about $40,000 in profit. Within the same two year period, my credit was restored and my documentable income was better established. Another opportunity then presented itself: An improving market. I was working as a real estate agent in North Oxnard. A developer approached our real estate firm with an opportunity to sell twenty-four new townhomes known as Vineyard Gardens. The townhomes were built in an industrial area right along the freeway. The developer wanted our firm to sell them ASAP.

Positioned next to screaming cars and a dirty industrial park, this project was not exactly the hottest ticket in town. Finally, after being turned down by the other agents, the selling opportunity was offered to me. (I was the youngest and least experienced agent in the firm.) This was my hometown. The area was very familiar me. I accepted the contract, with a single stipulation: I wanted to be the exclusive selling agent. The firm's broker granted the request, and I began selling the new project.

The developer had built a wall blocking off the view of the industrial park, which minimized the awareness that it was next door. The development itself had charm and romance— it was actually inviting. The only obstacle remaining was its location next to the freeway. I realized that there was a specific target audience for these townhomes—commuters who left for work early and drove some distance to their jobs. We just needed to connect with them and get them inside the development. The townhomes were "very sexy." ("Very sexy" is, of course, technical, professional real estate terminology.)

With "luxury homes located in a growing community with easy freeway access" as the main selling point, every single unit was sold and closed within 6 months. As a bonus, I made enough money for a 5% down payment, and I qualified for a new loan. I was able to purchase one of the "very sexy" townhomes myself! Once again, seeing value where no one else did paid off. Learning to look for hidden value is one of the most valuable assets to making great real estate purchases and acquiring sustainable wealth and lasting income.

Today, I live in Temecula Valley with my lovely wife, Renee. We live in a beautiful home overlooking The Temecula Wine Country. I entered the real estate business in 1978, specializing in real estate sales and marketing, and mortgage banking. I have also built eighteen homes.

After I sold that little beach front condominium, I began to develop the ability to assess my skills, assets, potential and character. This tool of self assessment has allowed me to better position myself, and make profitable decisions.

I am the broker of Harvest Team, Inc. and two other real estate companies in Temecula, California. My sales and marketing team is flourishing. Throughout my career, I have negotiated, brokered, and closed approximately 2,000 transactions for many satisfied clients. Specializing in real estate sales and marketing in Southern California, I have had the privilege to recruit and/or work with over eighty wonderful real estate agents and associates. I've become a competitive leader in the real estate industry as well as a student of South California real estate market trends.

My life is good because of strong faith, careful strategies, positive vision and strong determination. I equate my life to a Monopoly board: I made the choice to rise beyond simply passing Go and collecting a small $200 paycheck.

My passion and mission is to help other people do the same. In order to do this, self- assessment and the desire to reinvent or reestablish yourself is a must. It is never too late to begin or start over. It all begins with asking the question: "Why should I settle for a small allowance each time I 'pass go' and collect a token paycheck?" You could own Park Place and New York Avenue, own hotels and collect rent, and own the railroads and utilities!

All you have to do is recognize who you are, understand the value of what you have and learn what to look for. You can transform what you currently have into something of greater value. It can be done by anyone with the right vision, attitude and drive. Consider this your invitation to be that person and begin a new journey today! Discover what you want—and why you want it.

This book, "Reviving the American Dream in Southern California: How to Purchase A Home and Pay It Off In Five Years," contains nine very simple chapters. I lay out traditional, time tested, proven strategies for purchasing real estate, paying it off sooner, and developing sustainable wealth and lasting income.

My 35 year professional real estate career and life story are woven throughout the book. I use these stories to highlight what to do and what not to do—what works and what doesn't. Learn from my successes and benefit even more from my mistakes. If you follow these strategies, you will accelerate your real estate wealth learning by ten to thirty years. It is a fast read and a life's journey. Please join me.

Chapter 1   How to Buy Your Home

Chapter 2   Know Exactly What You Want

Chapter 3   Why Own? What to Know About Ownership

Chapter 4   Making More Money

Chapter 5   Reinventing and Reestablishing Yourself

Chapter 6   Health and Wellness in Real Estate

Chapter 7   Purchasing Investment Property

Chapter 8   Why Southern California

Chapter 9   A Go to Guide, Links, References and Networks

I invite you to join me on this journey. If you want more information about me and my wealth-building strategies, please visit **www.SouthernCaliforniaRealEstateSystem.com** or **www.LloydMize.com.**

CHAPTER 1

HOW TO PURCHASE YOUR HOME

More than likely, you are reading my book because you want to live the American Dream: Purchase a home you love, call it your own and pay it off. But the dream comes with a lot of questions: Where do you begin? Do you start with a real estate agent? Do you wait until you have all the money in place? How much money do you need? What kinds of homes are available? What if all the money is not there? Will the market go up or down if you wait? How do interest rates affect your purchasing power?

The question I receive the most is, "How can it be possible to buy a home and pay it off in five years? This has to be a gimmick or trick." You can do it! The strategies I lay out in this book are time tested and proven. It is common knowledge, but not commonly used. They are very simple to follow, and can be tailored to fit your specific wants and desires.

These are all great questions, ones that most new and recurring homebuyers have, or should have. When most people get to the issue of money, their dreams become stifled. If this is you, remember my Surfside III condominiums story: I had no money, no reasonably good credit or documentable income, for that purchase. All I had was potential and a dream. But that did not mean waiting around until I had answers to all the above questions

Mindset: Prepare, Pace and Pursue
Before I even briefed my friend on the deal, I gathered as much information as possible on the listing and local real estate market trends. Looking at market trends, and the other properties that had sold around it, I could predict that appreciation was likely. Since I had done my homework, I was ready to purchase so that I could restart my real estate investment plans and build sustainable wealth and lasting income.

Presumably, you are ready to purchase as well, and looking for the right opportunity. Schedule an appointment with a real estate professional. Share what you want to accomplish. Ask what you need to do to accomplish your dream. Specifically, ask how they can assist. Regardless of what market you are looking in, what size home you are after, or how many people you need to accommodate, every real estate purchase will require a down payment, proof of reasonably good credit, and a documentable source of income. All 3 of the above are required for the approval of a mortgage or real estate loan to purchase.

As the listing real estate agent of a home for sale, the agent when reviewing offers from prospective buyers, will require an approval letter from the buyer's lender or bank. This is known in the industry as a "pre-approval" letter. No one wants to open escrow with a potential buyer who will not qualify for a new loan. Furthermore, no one wants to do business with someone who has not prepared beforehand by having their finances lined up. To be an effective home buyer you must figure out how you plan to finance your new home before seriously looking at and making offers on potential homes.

As demonstrated with the Surfside III purchase, there are other means to financing property if you are not financially ready. In that case, I brought on a partner. However, you'll need more than finances to be completely ready as a home buyer. You also need emotional intelligence. Being emotionally qualified is as significant as being financially qualified to purchase a home— and even more significant if you are determined to pay it off early.

What do I mean by emotional intelligence? Simply this: Emotions are an essential part of making decisions. Adopt a healthy mindset that creates confidence and peace with your vision, wants and desires. It is critical to have the right mindset and belief. Fully believe in your vision, plan and strategy. Before you even start to think about finances make sure that you have stability in your life. You don't want emotional strife to keep you from making intellectually sound decisions. We will thoroughly discuss aspects of emotional intelligence and what

I refer to as "moving forward with certainty" throughout the 9 chapters of this book.

You also need to use your intellect. You will need to make sharp, informed decisions. Become keenly aware of your market place. Know market trends. Research comparable sales data to the properties you are most interested in. (Your real estate agent is a good resource for this.) Also, within this book I have provided additional links, references and networks that are a huge resource for Southern California real estate. It is important to know the local current market, as well as overall real estate market trends.

Even if you are emotionally sound and financially capable, if you don't know the facts, you can't make wise decisions. An occasional lucky guess can work out, but you can't build sustainable wealth based on luck. We want certainty and positive results.

Avoid drama at all cost. Stress will overwhelm you if you are not ready. Instead, invest the time to create your own steps and be prepared. Get your life and data in order. Then schedule an appointment with a professional you trust to educate you on the latest market trends and what they mean. (In chapter 9 of this book, I have provided a link that will help you find a real estate professional in your area.) Before your appointment with a real estate professional, take the time to do your own research. Make an effort to gain a general understanding of your market. That allows you to ask educated questions and get the real help required to make a successful home purchase.

THE SOUTHERN CALIFORNIA MARKET

As the market changes, prices move up and down. In Southern California, since the 1950s real estate values have risen, meaning that for sixty plus years homes in Southern California have appreciated. Depending on the region and the agency reporting, the last thirty years, homes have appreciated an average of 2.5 to 5% equity growth annually. Some years there is no gain. Some years show a 20% increase. Some years have large value corrections and downturns. But overall, property values increase an estimated 2.5% to 5% annually.

If there is a shortage of housing, a seller can ask for a higher price. If there are more sellers in the real estate market than buyers, prices will tend to move down. Interest rates are another factor: When rates are low, prices have a tendency to move up, and vice versa. In the late 1970s and into the 1980s, interest rates were so high that it created a very sluggish real estate market. As interest rates began to ease to affordable levels in 1986 and 1987, a real estate boom was created. Values went to all-time highs.

Knowing the market equips you with the knowledge you need in order to settle on a fair price, for both you and the seller. Rounding large figures to the nearest thousand, we can look at the Southern California real estate market and gain some knowledge of how it has worked over the course of several years.

At the time of this publication, the market is in recovery mode and the country is moving beyond the "Great Recession" of

2007 and 2008. The recession began in 2007 with real estate values beginning to decline as early as 2006. By 2008, the market had completely crashed, which leveled and corrected real estate prices. As a result, the government made corrections to federal monetary policy, and interest rates dropped to all-time lows. A buyer's market was created.

Jump ahead to 2009 and the "Great Recession" hit bottom. Real estate leveled off, then gradually started to increase in Southern California regions. In 2009, the median home value leveled off in Southern California. (In some areas the median home price fell to as low as $250,000.) In the same year, in some regions, home values increased as much as 10%. The year 2010 saw another 10% increase.

This type of research is very easy to find. Simply Google "median home values in Southern California." Easy math shows us that a home that leveled off in 2009 to a value of $250,000 would be valued at $302,500 by the end of 2010. That's a gain of $52,500!

An interesting side note is that in 2010, the mainline media was still gasping and asking, "When will the real estate market ever hit bottom?" The reality was it did hit bottom the year before, and in some areas, it climbed back by 20%. The point is, do your own simple, generalized research. Don't believe everything that gets reported in the media.

I am not advocating that, "Now is the perfect time to buy a home." Furthermore, just because the media and the general public are giddy about "buying a home now" suggesting it may be a buyer's market does not mean it is necessarily true. My 35 years of professional real estate experience has convinced me that it is always the perfect time to buy a home as long as you are ready.

If you understand the market and know your purchasing power, your home is waiting for you. Connect with a trusted real estate professional that can help you keep track of the market trends and stay informed on what is available. Look for and expect the right purchasing opportunities to come your way. Know with certainty you are in control. Again, Chapter 9 will help you with market research.

QUALIFYING FOR A MORTGAGE, BOTH FINANCIALLY AND EMOTIONALLY

Though real estate lending is readily available, your purchasing power depends on your comfort level with monthly mortgage payments, your finances and credit worthiness. Like my favorite board game, whether you have a monopoly on specific properties with hotels, the railroad companies, or you just collect $200 as you pass Go, always know what you qualify for financially.

In order to be approved for a home loan, you need documentable income, reasonably good credit; and a down payment. Good income does not necessarily mean making a million dollars a year. Generally if your total monthly debt is

40-50% of your gross income you have good income. Usually lenders require a two year history of level or increasing income with your job or business.

Income

The total monthly debt I mentioned above refers to principal and interest payments in order to pay the mortgage off over a period of time. This period of time is known as amortization. If the loan is amortized over thirty years, at the end of thirty years the loan will be paid off. To shorten the amortization to fifteen years or less the principal payments increase. We will get into more detail later as we discuss paying your home off in five years.

In addition to the principal and interest payments, real estate taxes and property insurance are also included. The total real estate payment includes principal, interest, taxes and insurance, commonly referred to as PITI. If the PITI monthly payment is $2,000, lender guidelines require a gross monthly income of $6,000, based on a 40% income to debt ratio. Gross monthly income can be as low as $4,000 if the income to debt ratio increases to 50%.

Credit

With respect to credit, people with a FICO score of over 640 are usually considered to have reasonably good credit. Lenders usually do not want to see any foreclosures or bankruptcies in the last three years. Also, few, if any, thirty day late payments are allowed within the last twelve months. Of course, there are exceptions to every guideline.

Tiffany Hazelaar is the owner of Dedicated Credit Repair located in Southern California. Tiffany offers a bit more credit advice in Chapter 5, "Reinventing Yourself". For now I would like to introduce you to Tiffany:

"Dedicated Credit Repair is an incredibly valuable resource to lenders, Realtors® and clients who have a hunger for accurate credit advice. That's why we treat every credit file as if it were our own. You will find the walls of our office lined with recent testimonials from lenders, Realtors® and past clients who have raved about our services.

We can help Clients in all FICO Score ranges. Lower FICO scores can be boosted by a range of 60-90 points in a time frame of three to six months, when all the required steps are followed. We provide consultations as well as client status reports via phone, webinar or Skype to accommodate our clients all over the U.S".

Down Payment

Finally you need a down payment, which can be as little as 3.5% of the purchase price. For qualified member of the military, VA benefits offer zero down payment programs. With good income, reasonably good credit, it is easy to obtain real estate financing.

I've asked Bill Provost to explain the value of pre-qualifying for a mortgage. He offers several tips on how to begin the qualifying process for real estate finance. Bill is a mortgage banker based in Southern California and is an expert with respect to real estate financing. His link is provided for quick and easy loan qualification guidelines and calculations. You will find links to many helpful people who can help you throughout the property buying process when you go to:

www.SouthernCaliforniaRealEstateSystem.com or
www.LloydMize.com.

Bill Provost:

"One of the major reasons Lloyd is such a great resource to his real estate clients is because of his background in real estate. In addition to his many years as a Realtor®, Lloyd also has twenty-five years of experience as an accomplished mortgage lender. This gives him a big advantage over most real estate agents.

A good reliable pre-approval letter is extremely important in today's real estate market. Once an initial financial assessment is completed and your purchasing power is established, you have negotiating leverage and intellectual strength to pursue your ultimate purchase. The "pre-approval process" should be very thorough so that you as a prospective purchasing client are taken serious and respected by the real estate agent you choose. That means you can effectively shop for a home and have absolute confidence that your loan will have no issues.

While mortgage lending has gone through some very big changes over the past four to five years one thing hasn't changed, the knowledge and accomplished expertise which Lloyd approaches the real estate market to deliver dependable and up to date decisions for his clients that they can count on."

Qualifying Financially and Emotionally

There may be a difference in the loan amount you qualify for, and the amount you are comfortable with. For example, your income and credit history may indicate that you qualify for a loan with a $2,000 monthly payment. But you only feel comfortable with a payment of $1,700. In order to lower your payment to a point where it fits your emotional qualifications, you will need to pursue one or more strategies.

One strategy is to increase the amount of your down payment. This decreases the amount of your loan, which will be reflected in your monthly payment. Another option is to pursue a lower loan amount. This, of course, will reduce your monthly payment. Perhaps you qualify financially for a $275,000 loan, but the payments will cause you emotional stress. For you, the best option may be to find a home you can purchase with a $255,000 loan, and its lower payments. The point here is that you need to find a loan amount you can handle financially and emotionally. You shouldn't pursue one without the other.

Also keep in mind that your monthly payments are more than just your loan amount. Your payment will also include your home insurance, as well as your local property taxes. Those amounts can vary from house to house, and from county to county. Your real estate professional can give you a pretty good idea of how insurance and taxes will affect your overall monthly payments.

Interest Rates on the Move:

If mortgage rates go up, you can quickly calculate what that does to your purchasing power. There is an amortization link in my website that will calculate payments by selecting different interest rates. For now make a note: Based on the $289,500 mortgage at 3.5% if rates move up 1% to 4.5%, the payment increases monthly by $167. If you maintain the same monthly payment as the 3.5% rate of $1,300, the loan balance supported with an interest rate of 4.5% drops from $289,500 to $256,570, a $33,000 drop in purchasing power. Be aware of the impact interest rates have over your purchasing power.

The Power of Pre-payment: It's a Mindset!

Let me show you the simple genius of pre-payment. For an example, we're going to look at a thirty year mortgage with a total PITI monthly payment of $1,696. To pay this off in five years is easy and simple; it is only a matter of making larger payments. Oh, I can hear you saying, "You've got to be kidding me! You've gone all this way to finally state the obvious." I hear you, but stay with me: There is more and I promise it gets exciting and powerful.

As a matter of fact, financially, emotionally and mentally what comes next through the entire balance of these 9 chapters is rewarding. It will be a huge "A-ha" moment! It is so much more than a formula to pay your home of sooner rather than later with the five year plan.

However, be warned, it is not for everyone. But it is available and achievable to anyone. It's a mindset: Know what you want. Know why you want it. The strategies, action steps and results will unfold. About 30% of our Southern California community is ready for this message, but only 20% of those people are ready to take action. Are you ready? You can be, and why not? You are in control of you.

Schedules Early Payoff:
We will go into more detail later, but for now using a $300, 000 purchase price model with only 3.5% down the total monthly PITI payment is $1,696. The loan balance is $289,500. Using the same interest rate of 3.5% take a look at the schedule below for other amortization terms

- 25 year payoff the total monthly PITI = $1,845; Additional Monthly payment = $149 or additional annual payment = $1,788

- Twenty year payoff the total monthly PITI = $2,075; Additional Monthly payment = $379 or additional annual payment = $4,548

- Fifteen year payoff the total monthly PITI = $2,465; Additional Monthly payment = $769 or additional annual payment = $9,235

- Ten year payoff the total monthly PITI = $3,258; Additional Monthly payment = $1,562 or additional annual payment = $18,752

- Five year payoff the total monthly PITI = $5,662; Additional Monthly payment = $3,966 or additional annual payment = $47,598

Let's Regroup and Gather Ourselves:

At first look the amortization chart can be overwhelming, but stay with me on this. At this point all that matters is getting your foot in the door. Or to use another one of my favorite sports analogies, get possession of the ball and then work on moving it downfield and across the goal line.

How much you are willing to pay each month will translate into the value of the home you purchase and how quick you pay it off based on the amortization term you choose. Remember our goal is to build wealth and lasting income, stay focused on your vision, wants and dreams.

How much you can spend monthly and annually circles back to knowing the value of what you have. Understanding your purchasing power will help you find the best property you want to afford. This is more powerful than what you can afford. Sometimes the amount is smaller but most of the time it is a larger value. With a ready knowledge of your real estate market, you will know how much you need and begin to develop a plan and strategy to create a budget and mindset to pay your home off in five years. We are on a journey. It is a process that is fully achievable. Stay focused and continually remind yourself what your life will look like once your home is paid off. You will be amazed! The possibilities are endless and they are waiting for you.

Before moving on to strategies to create early payoff and equity in property there is a technical and logistical piece of purchasing a home we should discuss, escrow. What the heck is escrow? The term is thrown around a lot, 'we just closed escrow' or 'once escrow is opened'. Aaron Lloyd gives us one of the best definitions of what escrow is and the significance it has to a successful home purchase. He is the president of Sunset One Escrow based in Southern California.

"So after you find that perfect home, you're Real Estate Agent is going to mention 'escrow'. This is where most Buyers and Sellers become the most curious. What is escrow? Believe it or not, this is one of the most common questions I am asked. Simply put, escrow is a disinterested (and licensed) neutral third-party which holds funds and/or collateral pending the completion of the terms of an agreement or contract. Most commonly implemented in Real Estate as a security for Buyers/Sellers/Lenders, Escrow may also be utilized for the transfer of high-value personal property (such as jewelry, boats, aircraft, mobile-homes, etc.),

child-adoptions, interests in a corporation, intellectual property or the purchase or sale of a business.

Historically speaking, escrow was originally adopted by merchants in France and England as a safeguard against theft, embezzlement and non-performance. Today, Escrow performs the same function but with the added benefit of surety bonds, fidelity policies and the like.

During the Great Depression (1934), escrow became formally institutionalized in the United States under "Mortgage Payment Escrows". Mortgage Payment escrows were a means of safeguarding the interest of the homeowners' and mortgage lenders. As is true today, most property tax amounts exceeded the normal monthly income of the homeowner and failure to pay them would subject the property to forfeit at the behest of the local/state/federal government. The solution was to allow the homeowner to pay in smaller, more manageable amounts over time, and defer the responsibility of paying the bill, on time, to the mortgage lender. This compromise provided assurance to the homeowner and lender that their respective interests were secure.

Over time the complexity of agreements began to require the legal expertise of attorneys. Since an attorney is employed by one of the principals, no one could fully trust the other to act impartially while control rested in the hands of the other.

Many states continue to require the services of an attorney to transfer real property. While understandable, albeit unnecessary, that number has been on the decline in recent years as regulation and commerce have demanded impartial, trusted, experienced, third-parties. California, well versed in legal precedent and a common front-runner for change, decided long ago that a legal representative employed by a principal cannot constitute an impartial third-party. As a response to the increasing problems associated with real property transactions the State provided the means for a regulated and licensed "Escrow Agent".

In California there are three different types of escrow companies. The first, being the strictest and most reliable, is the "Independent Escrow Agent". The nuances and differences are too many to be listed here. For a clear explanation as to the differences please visit our website.
You can find Sunset Escrow through Lloyd's site
www.SouthernCaliforniaRealEstateSystem.com or
www.LloydMize.com.

The selection of escrow is every bit as important as the selection of your Real Estate professional. The right escrow company can make all the difference."

Let's keep moving forward with certainty strategies to purchasing and paying your home off sooner than later.

CHAPTER 2

KNOW EXACTLY WHAT YOU WANT OUT OF A HOME

N ow you have determined your qualifying parameters both financially and emotionally. Also, the philosophy of paying your home off sooner rather than later is starting to soak in. I've discovered that once the reality of all this becomes a familiar concept, many other opportunities magically begin to line up.

As an example, in 2012 Renee and I were pursuing the purchase of a new home. Our preferred buying range capped at approximately $450,000. However, emotionally we were attracted to homes priced from $650,000 to $750,000. Once we realized where we stood, we began working on a budget to determine how much monthly income we would need to make a purchase in the higher range. We also figured out how much additional cash would be required to pay a home off over a five year time line. The more we worked with the concept, creative opportunities began to open up that allowed us to begin making adjustments within our businesses that would make the purchase a reality. I will follow up with more on that particular story later.

Now, back to you. The question is: What exactly do you want out of a home? Close your eyes and dream as big as you can. Remember that acquiring property is important as an investment. It allows you shelter and financial security for the rest of your life. It also becomes an asset you will pass on to your family or favorite charity. (After all, you cannot take it with you.)

If money was not a factor and there were no other obstacles, what would your ideal home look like? What kind of space would it have? Do you want a neighborhood community? If you have children, how are the schools in the area? Are there enough recreational activities to satisfy you? Start the process by figuring out exactly what you want. Then apply the limitations of reality. Regardless of your purchasing power or emotional intelligence, you must determine what you want and why it turns you on, so to speak, before you can make a great decision for your home purchase.

Once you know what you want, you can find a home within your purchasing ability that meets your standards. What if that home does not exist within your value range? Keep this truth in mind: The clearer you become about your dream home, the more opportunities show up.

What if the home you want is outside of your purchasing power at the moment? Use the tool of structural tension. Structural tension opens the door to creative thinking and achievement. It can be used for acquiring real estate, building business, improving relationships, sculpting your ideal body or planning an extravagant vacation.

Here is the basic idea of structural tension: Take blank piece of paper. At the bottom of the page, draw a line. That is the Current Reality you find yourself in. At the top of the page, draw another line. That represents your Desired Outcome. Where do you want to be at the end of this process? Now, in the middle of the page, fill in your strategies and plans that will help you go from where you are to where you want to be. Be creative! Set timetables and goals that will help you pull your Current Reality in line with your Desired Outcome.

As an example, let's say you want to buy a home. The price point has been established but what is available on the market does not match your price point. So you current realty is an affordability level of $300,000, while your ideal outcome is a home that is currently priced at $400,000.

At bottom of the page draw a line that is titled Current Reality = Home price point $300,000. At the top of the page draw another line titled Desired Outcome = Purchase a home priced at $400,000 with all my ideal features and amenities. Now in between, write action steps. Strategies will begin to take shape. As they do fill them in. Then begin to place ideal timelines to the steps and strategies. Picture a giant rubber band linking the Current Reality line to the Desired Outcome line, pulling them closer together.

Review your newly created structural tension chart daily and update the actions steps, strategies and timelines assigned to them. Magic begins to happen. You will see the more you review and update your chart, the tension on the rubber band will begin to pull your current reality to your desired outcome. Opportunities will show up that you would have otherwise missed.

Remember the Surfside III condominiums in Ventura County? With no income, down payment or credit, that condo was well outside of my purchasing power. I had to get creative. Since the purpose of purchasing this property was to eventually sell it for a profit, the opportunity to invite an outside investor as a partner opened up and we acquired the property.

Decide what your top priorities are for your ideal home and make it a point to fill as many of them as you can with a home within your purchasing power. For example, if a larger lot is a top priority, consider a smaller home on a larger lot. In the case of Renee and myself, it was more important to have a larger home and compromise with the lot size. Ultimately, we want both but for now a larger home is more important than a large lot.

Options are always in your favor. If large acreage is more important, consider moving to a more rural area where land prices are a better value than in urban areas. Another very good option is to purchase a premium vacant lot and place an affordable, comfortable manufactured home on the property until enough cash or income is available to build your ultimate home.

Moving to a more rural Southern California community can be a great option to achieve your perfect home. Creativity is one of your best allies and options to realizing your ideal home. In 1999 we lived in Ventura County. The average price of a home we wanted was in the $650,000. On vacation, traveling south on Interstate 15 South on our way to Mexico we discovered Temecula, California. We found similar homes and a "like-kind community" in Temecula, where homes were valued from $250,000 to $350,000.

Renee and I become intrigued. Temecula offered a family community, great schools, recreation, a thriving business community and the same fantastic weather we enjoyed in the Thousand Oaks region. We recognized the opportunity to relocate our real estate business from Thousand Oaks to Temecula, maintain our level of income and life style and reduce our housing expense by approximately 50%. It took five years of planning before we relocated, but in doing so we doubled our purchasing power.

The Surfside III condo is another example of created opportunity. Within two years the investment provided a handsome profit. That meant additional purchasing power for me. In addition, my credit was restored and I was able to make it around the Monopoly board enough times to establish documentable income.

Again the Vineyard Garden Townhomes in 1986 provided a great opportunity to purchase more real estate and develop income. From 1988 to 1990, I accumulated about thirteen properties.

The market is fickle

Acquiring property is one step. The next is keeping it and developing a plan to pay it off as soon as possible. Always stay focused your primary goals, wants and desires. Beware of shifting sands and changing economic trends.

In 1989: Market values peaked. I did not know it at the time or expect it to change so quickly. I had just sold a property that we purchased in 1987. We profited by approximately $100,000. We were on a roll!! We invested our $100,000 into our dream home, which we purchased for $435,000. It was a new home located in a fantastic community on a one acre parcel. Perfect!

We loved it so much! I knew within twelve to eighteen months the value would be approximately $650,000. But in 1990, not only did the market peak, it stopped. We were stuck with big payments and huge negative cash flow from the thirteen properties we accumulated from 1986 to 1989. We (actually, it's I, because as Renee points out, this was all my brilliant planning) had over-leveraged, meaning we had bought too many properties with very limited down payments, which created high PITI payments.

The rent we collected on average left a negative cash flow ranging from $200 to $500 per property. We had to painfully liquidate all of our property to keep up, including our dream home. It was the very last property we finally sold in 1995 for $385,000. It took us five years to liquidate. Remarkably, we maintained our good credit status. The market can change and turn on a dime. Beware of the always-changing market trends. Do not be caught with negative cash flows and too many properties. Stay focused on your investment strategies and be disciplined in spending habits.

I was at Disneyland in 1995, when I got the news that our last property had sold. By 1997, I was back in a position to purchase. I wanted to get back onto a one-acre parcel and into a 2,000 square foot home. With most properties priced at over $650,000 and my purchasing power at about $450,000, it was time to get creative, again.

A tiny two bedroom, one bath property in Newbury Park, California, built in 1966, sat on a lot surrounded by larger lot parcels. It wasn't even close to a one acre lot, and the house was only 875 square feet. It was way under my ideal. I brought Renee to view the property and tried hard to share the potential I envisioned with her. When we arrived, I had to strongly encourage Renee just to get her out of the car and go inside the house. She reluctantly went in and came out in less than a minute, exclaiming, "You have got to be kidding me! I couldn't even fit my shoes into that house." However, with a beautiful location, great neighborhood with custom houses down the block, and an 8,000 square foot lot, I knew this house could be rebuilt into a 2,000 square foot home, complete with a swimming pool. After watching the red Southern California sun sink behind our property, Renee was on board as well.

It was a 30 year-old home. We purchased it for $150,000. We borrowed about $205,000 and spent a total of $250,000 to do a major remodel. We added square footage, complete with a fantastic outdoor living area which included a Pebble-Tech pool and spa surrounded with colored stamped concrete and soft landscape. With the backdrop of the Conejo Ridge, pine trees and redwood decks that accented the home, it was gorgeous. Most important, it was a lot of fun to live in. We created about $200,000 in equity. The value at the time of completion was approximately $600,000.

The Power of Interior Design and Remodeling

Deanne Marie, Smart Solutions for Busy People, is an expert in the field of decorating and remodeling. She consults with home owners about creatively taking your home from "drabs to a dream", same home with professional design and creation. Deanne is very good at this, feel free to connect with Deanne through my website which is posted throughout the book.

Deanne offers this, "Congratulations on making the leap to one of the most important purchases of your life! Many homeowners are overwhelmed after move-in day, thinking "now what?" Then it's time to make your house into the place you call home—a haven where you can bring together your family and friends to connect and celebrate. I can help! I'm Deanne Marie and I believe that home decorating is more than putting a pillow on a sofa, or shopping to fill your home with "stuff." It's a process, and one that rewards you with a space that represents you and welcomes you back every time you enter. Because as you create the beautiful, comfortable home of your dreams, you're also creating the foundation to build and nurture lasting, meaningful relationships with the people you love."

Idealize your standards, then create the possibilities yourself for them to be reached. Buying a $150,000 home when you want a $500,000 home is not settling. Become clear on what your ideal home is. Then lay out a plan to achieve it. Begin with a structural tension chart showing your current reality and desired outcome. As you review it daily, fill in strategies, action steps and timelines. Watch in amazement as your current reality draws closer to your desired outcome.

Deciding exactly what you want allows you to know which priorities are an absolute must for you to be happy in your home. From the size of the closets and the number of bedrooms to the layout of the property and the orientation of the lot, knowing what you are after will open you up to more options.

You can then see what is available and what can be made to fit your standards. Never settle! Look for a home that has your most important features, and that has the potential to be modified to reach your ultimate goals. With a determined will and a little creativity, you can achieve the kitchen layout, great room, closest space and other amenities you most desire.

In the next chapter, I will begin laying out the foundation regarding the significance of owning your home free and clear. Why is it important? What do you need to know?

CHAPTER 3

WHY OWN AND WHAT TO KNOW

Let's take a step back now and review the necessary steps to successfully purchasing your home. Know the value of what you have, and what your purchasing power is. This will set the price range for the properties you want to seek out. Once you know where you are, the value of what you have, and your ideal outcome, you can use the structural tension chart to create the action steps to achieve what you want.

Next, study the market trends in your local area. Include homes that are available for sale, as well as homes that have sold recently. Once you've done that, it is time to set an appointment with a trusted real estate professional. All this is the foundation for paying your home off in five years—first you must purchase it. Start with a home that has the most amenities within the price range you have set. Then apply creativity to transform the home to fit your standards by the time you pay it off.

What is the value of homeownership? Understand that in my thinking, homeownership means no mortgage. Having a mortgage means that the bank owns your home and, until you pay if off, you are paying rent to the bank. Once your house it paid off, your home is yours and your life is opened to a whole new level of opportunity. Of course, purchasing a home and paying it off in five years requires discipline and stubborn commitment.

Eliminating your home mortgage will eliminate the largest monthly debt people carry all their lives. Having no monthly mortgage debt propels you into a realm of evolved financial freedom. Now, you may hear that many financial advisors recommend maintaining a mortgage makes sense financially. That is absolutely crazy. Eliminate the debt! Be debt free!

A mortgage does not have to be a thirty-year or more commitment. The faster you pay it off, the sooner you can set money aside for retirement, investments, vacations, and other recreational expenses. Purchasing a home and making it yours is a tangible asset and wealth builder. Benefits like these can only be enjoyed once you own your home, and not the bank. Keep your eye on the ball. Avoid becoming comfortable with a thirty-year mortgage, spending money on nonessential and unnecessary things, and losing sight of the goal to own your home. Trust me, I know.

After completing the major remodel to our own Thousand Oaks mini-resort, a recurring dream to own a 3,000-plus square foot home on a five-acre parcel in rural Southern California was renewed. When we discovered Temecula in 1999 we really liked what we saw. We decided that we could have a great future there. If you remember what I said in the previous chapter, we could live in the same home for half the price of what we could buy in Ventura county. The family, community and business opportunities were equal to (if not greater than) that in Ventura County. The Temecula region completely captivated our real estate interests.

At the time, a ten-acre parcel of land cost anywhere from $200,000 to $600,000 in Thousand Oaks. That same parcel of land could be bought in the Temecula area from as low as $40,000, to an average of $150,000. The opportunity was available to purchase four, five-to-ten acre parcels. My goal was to build, what I called, a "like kind" economic base in the Inland Empire that would allow me to bring my real estate business with me while maintaining my income level and doubling my purchasing power.

In 2001, I purchased a ten-acre parcel just outside of Temecula. I acquired three other five-acre parcels from 2001 to 2004. My plan was to develop 3,000 square foot homes to sell for a profit over a three to four year span so that I could pay off my own home. By 2007, my expectation was to have my home paid off and my retirement funded.

The Temecula Valley wine country is a thriving member of California's fourteen other wine regions. Geographically, it is located within an hour of both the beach and the mountains. Also, it is an hour drive to beautiful San Diego, Orange County's Irvine and Newport Beach, and one of our favorite playgrounds, Palm Desert. This area of Southern California presented a perfect building opportunity.

Like my little beach condo in 1984, I could sense this was a great opportunity and a great challenge. Once again, I recognized the need for an investor/partner. A business colleague and good friend shared my vision for this project. Together, we acquired property and began to build houses. From 2001 to 2004, we acquired a total of six investment lots. We began building houses in 2005. We sold our first one in 2006 for 1.4 million dollars, which gave us a very handsome profit of $377,000. We were on a roll!

We were convinced we were on the right path. Unfortunately, the roll was downhill from there. The market shifted once again in 2006 and 2007, and we could not sell four of the investment properties. Seeming to mirror 1990 to 1995, all of the proprieties had to be liquidated from 2008 to 2010 at painful losses.

Despite the advantages of Southern California and Temecula, equity growth and wealth in real estate typically involves steady plodding and focus. Usually, it is not an overnight success. The success enjoyed from our real estate and building business from 2002 to 2006 seemed to be sustainable—it was not. With the increased income and cash flow, I purchased additional properties. I moved too fast to build out the investment lots. In hindsight, it would have been better to build one home at a time, sell it, and move to the next. In addition, we spent too much money on nonessential recreational toys such as 2 motorcycles and a motorhome.

We had built and sold 18 homes by 2007. But when the market shifted, we still had four investment homes to sell. Plus, I had a $575,000 mortgage on my own beautiful 3,000 square foot home on 10 acres. I loved that home, but I quickly realized that settlement and liquidation was my only option. I had spent too much and had too much real estate for a downward market.

Owning your own home means security. When the banks own your home that security is unavailable to you. On the cusp of success, the Great Recession hit and stopped me and my partner in our tracks.

We invested all we had to purchase lots and build investment properties. For our investment/building strategy to be profitable, the new homes needed to sell in a range of $675,000 to $750,000. The recession had rapidly depreciated the prices of the homes. By 2009, the remaining properties were sold, but at a great loss. They only sold for $250,000 to about $350,000 for each home. I lost my motorhome and motorcycles to appease the bank. My partner lost even more, including his personal health.

Once again, my credit was shot and I was left with nowhere to go but up. There is a time and place for spending on personal luxuries. While you are trying to pay off a home is not one of those times or places. My old friends, Miguel and Lupita Castillo, understand this, and did not make the same mistakes I did. With steady plodding, they keep their focus on owning and paying off not only their home, but all of their investment properties.

In the late 1980s and early 1990s they wisely chose to place all of their home and investment properties on fifteen year mortgages. They made the sacrifice of doing without the nonessential toys and made the choice of accelerating all of their mortgages, paying them off. Now they enjoy substantial and sustainable income. Maintaining that focus, they completely funded their retirement. Now Miguel and Lupita are pursuing their life passion, sailing around the world in their "Free and clear" sailboat.

"Free and clear" home ownership is the foundation to acquiring wealth and sustainable income. Rather than spending your income on a monthly mortgage, you are free to direct that money to other significant wealth and income builders such as investments, businesses or education.

Once your home purchase is made, paying it off in five years begins by developing the right mind set. The purchase begins with an affordable and manageable 30, 20 or possibly a fifteen-year mortgage. However, if your vision and plan is to build wealth and sustainable income sooner rather than later, you need to quickly develop the "Free and clear" mind-set. Adjust your belief from a thirty-year payoff to a five-year plan.

It all begins with believing you can. Think in terms of "sooner rather than later." Slice and dice to cut twenty to tweinty-five years off the traditional mind set of retiring after thirty to thirty-five years of long, hard employment. Why settle for the traditional thirty-year-plan? Owning your home in five years is the first step to becoming a 45-year-old, or younger, retiree and becoming financially independent. You may be in your 50s or 60s reading this and thinking, "Ugh, it's too late for me!" The truth is that now is a great time to establish new ways of believing, and take action. It is never too late!

Once you've made your purchase, maintain focus with stubborn discipline and commitment. Envision yourself paying off your home in five years. Doing so will create investment purchasing power and financial freedom. Refer often to the amortization schedule to keep in mind the additional monthly and annual dollar amount required to pay off the unwanted mortgage.

There is more good news. The savings are huge. Using an example of a $300,000 mortgage, paying it off in five years rather than 30 years will save you approximately $103,170. It takes more cash to accelerate the early payment, however there are three life-changing benefits.

The first is the freeing of disposable income after the mortgage is paid in full. The second is the huge savings: $103,170 in the example I used above. But the really big benefit comes from creating the mindset and lifestyle of making substantially more income, what I call the "Entrepreneurial Mindset."

The American Dream is about owning your property—but it includes so much more. The privilege and freedom to create and own your own business is the spine of America. America is built on and thrives on successful businesses created by independent entrepreneurs. Now more than any other time in the history of our great nation, Americans need encouragement to break away and truly be financially independent. You can do it, through "Free and clear" property ownership and business ownership.

Owning your own business is absolutely the best way to be financially independent. Every year, people start new businesses that represent all types of industries, passions and needs in our economy. They are affordable and easy to begin. Working in tandem with your existing job, many new businesses can be started with a few hundred dollars, and a time investment of five to twenty hours a week. Within the first three to twelve months, businesses like these will produce a monthly financial reward ranging from an average of $1,000 to $3,000.

I know from solid personal experience: This is substantial and sustainable income that will easily pay your mortgage to ZERO! Chapter 4 discusses laying a foundation to making more money and pursuing business prosperity. Many web links and references are available through the balance of the chapters for business opportunities, coaching and references. Let's continue our Journey as we go around the "Monopoly Board" together and look at the limitless possibilities and opportunities.

CHAPTER 4

MAKING MORE MONEY

Shifting gears from the thirty year plan to a five year plan sets the stage for the next mindset change: Starting and building a business. This will allow you to make more money and increase sustainable income. The central theme of this book is how you can pay off your home in five years. We started with an affordable thirty-year mortgage, then shifted gears to show you how to pay it off in five years. The quickest way to purchase the home of your dreams and pay it off in five years is simple: Make more money.

When you make more money, your purchasing power increases. Capital is available to accelerate your mortgage payoff. You probably already work about forty to forty-five hours per week. The thought of trying to make more money may be overwhelming to consider...but you can do it! It is simply a process. This chapter is designed to break the process down into manageable action steps so you can achieve this goal.

Making more money is not about suffering through longer days at work. You want to replace hard work with smart work through developing your own business, allowing you to reap financial benefits. There are four keys to making money: 1.) time management, 2.) aligning with a community of like-minded people, 3.) establishing better relationships, and 4.) discovering new possibilities.

Remembering these four things and cultivating them equips you with skills to navigate your own economy. Understand that the economy is just a set of rules applied to relationships to serve people. The fact is, the economy is neither good nor bad, but rather it morphs and evolves. It just is. It always has the same amount of dollars and time in circulation. Money just shifts through the economy from person to person, and industry to industry.

The key is to track these shifts and look for opportunities to take advantage of them, creating a better "you-economy." If you keep up with the economy and educate yourself on patterns and trends, you can find a niche and exploit it to garner fantastic benefit.

Recently, many jobs have been lost and there have been thousands of failed businesses. But there are unlimited and unbelievable opportunities waiting patiently to be discovered. If you are prepared, practiced, and persistent those opportunities will become your ticket to success. Starting a successful business begins with proper preparation. Just as you need to educate and prepare yourself to purchase a home, starting a business requires you to be physically, emotionally, and intellectually prepared. Know this with certainty: You are more than enough and have more than enough resources to start your own business. Time, education, focus, and faith are all that is required.

First, I'm going to break down basic time-management strategies. When we talk about time most people respond, "I just don't have enough time and/or energy." But that just isn't true! We each have enough time to accomplish our dreams. (As for having enough energy, optimal health—a healthy mind and a healthy body—is essential.) This means feeling good, looking good, and thinking great in order to make the best decisions as opportunities unfold. You need to be a healthy person if you are going to run a successful business. We will explore the importance of optimal health and wellness in Chapter 6.)

To actualize paying off your home in five years, you will need to develop innovative methods of acquiring extra income. Many people are uncomfortable with the idea of developing a business as a means to extra income. Just the thought can be overwhelming, which is natural. However, it is quite easy, just follow the steps.

The first, and most comfortable step for most people, is to look for part-time employment that will fit with your full-time job.

Make it a point to only pursue part-time employment with two primary objectives. One, look for employment that is compatible with your interests. Place your efforts and energy into something you already enjoy. The other objective is to be clear within yourself that part-time employment is a means to an end. It is temporary.

Another important tip is to be realistic about your wage. Whether you get paid hourly or according to a set schedule, you need to learn what your time is worth, and expect to be compensated at the higher end of the "wage scale." Make sure that your compensation will eventually rise to a level that enables you to pay your home off in five years.

Remember that this is a journey, not a destination. It takes TIME and EFFORT, but it can be done. Your ultimate goal is not to have a part-time job. It is to develop your own business. Some will choose to skip over part-time employment and move right in to developing their own business. That's what we will talk about next.

You must discover the kind of market/business you want to enter, and how to position yourself. This is a fairly simple process. It just takes time and the right resources. By investing five to ten hours a week in your new business, you can quickly build an additional $1,000 to $3,000 a month, and grow exponentially from there.

TIME MANAGEMENT

Manage your time, rather than allowing your time to manage you. It is your time, after all. Everyone has the same amount of time every day—24 hours or 1,440 minutes. Every week, you have 168 hours to accomplish everything you can. Everyone has the same 168 hours.

Building a business plan begins with scheduling your time. Plan your time in weekly segments, with each day as a smaller segment. Start with days off and recreation, then lay out the essentials: Time to sleep, family time, time to work, etc. Do not schedule unrealistically. Make sure your schedule reflects your needs, goals, interests, and capabilities.

Once your schedule is set make sure you stick to it. Stay focused on your dream and the significance of your wants and desires. If you find your wants and desires are not that significant, that's OK. It's a natural part of the process. What then? You are on the right track, take out a piece of blank paper and ask yourself, "What do I want that holds significance in my life?" Don't wait! Just begin to write. I promise that the answer to your "significant want" will eventually unfold to you.

There are certain things that you absolutely have to do: Sleep, work, eat, and spend time with your family. If you sleep seven hours a day, that equals forty-nine hours per week. With a full-time, eight-hour a day job for five days per week, you rack up forty more hours from work. Add about two hours a day for making and eating food, and you have occupied about 103 hours out of your 168-hour week. This leaves you with about 65 hours for family time, health and wellness, church, hobbies, recreation, and other things. Even if you give five hours per day to your family, you still have about thirty hours left to build a better income for yourself. When you see it this way, you can imagine how and where you can apply five to twenty hours per week to begin a significant business, one that will make you about $1,000 to $3,000 per month within the first twelve months.

Let me encourage you to take a minute and schedule your life. Know what you want and the significance of what you want. This is sometimes called the "compelling why" behind the want. Commit to it and schedule it into your week. Execute what you have scheduled with effective action and certainty. Take an hour right now to investigate how you are spending your time. Remember that it is a journey, not a destination. Look at my schedule on the following page to use as a template. Then those five to twenty hours to devote to your new business that will provide you with additional income to pay off your home in five years.

LLOYD MIZE'S 168-HOUR WEEK

Sleep	7 hours x 7 days	49 hours
Day Job	8 hours x 5 days	40 hours
Family Time	4 hours x 7 days	28 hours
Exercise	2 hours x 3 days	6 hours
Church	1 hour x 5 days	5 hours
Personal Development /Marketing	2 hours x 3 days	6 hours
BNI/Social and Business Networks	2 hours x 3 days	6 hours
Toastmasters	2 hours x 3 days	6 hours
Dress, Prep, and Food	2 hours x 7 days	14 hours
Hobbies/Recreation	2 hours x 4 days	8 hours
		Total Hours = 168

For me, things like Toastmasters, personal development, marketing, BNI® and Business Networks are as much a part of my business as my personal life. The lines are blurred between the 2two I spend about 18 hours total on all of these combined. Devote as much time or more and watch your business grow, as well as your social and people skills.

In 2008, after the market had crashed yet again, I was broke and without credit. We needed to replace our $150,000 per year income. Falling back on my real estate knowledge, my forty-hour workweek was focused on my new real estate sales and marketing business, rather than my failed building and development business. I had to assess, adjust, and reinvent myself and my business. In this process, we kept on the lookout for other money making opportunities.

A year earlier, in 2007, Renee and I were both significantly overweight. We looked into a health coach system centered on Dr. Wayne Andersen's book, "Dr. A's Habits of Health." Within five months Renee had lost about sixty pounds. I had dropped forty pounds myself. We were so pleased with our new health and look. It was so easy, we just followed the coaching and easy steps. In the process of getting to our optimal weight, we discovered that there was a business side to Dr. Andersen's comprehensive health system.

Renee devoted about five to ten hours each week to becoming educated as a health coach. Over the next twelve months, a home-based business was developed that produced about $42,000 a year in 2008. The work included coaching health clients to their optimal weight and leads them into a healthier lifestyle. There is more to this story in Chapter 5 and 6, "Reinventing Yourself" and "Health and Wellness in Real Estate" and on our website as well:

www.SouthernCaliforniaRealEstateSystem.com or
www.LloydMize.com

During the real estate crash of 2008 we recognized our real estate building and development business was dead and gone. But we kept our minds open to other opportunities and options coming our way, based on our natural interests and passions.

Take time to identify industries that interest you. Become educated in these industries. Position yourself to start and build a potential clientele list. Hone your skills as a businessperson developing your business and social acumen. Develop your social networking skills. As you are starting your business and preparing yourself to make more money, social networking websites such as Facebook, Twitter, and LinkedIn will become an ally to bolster your success. Creating a web presence will connect you with a vast audience of potential customers who will be able to follow your every move, recommendations, products and services. Almost all these social sites are free to use and, at the very least, serve as free advertising to promote you and your company.

BUSINESS, RELATIONSHIPS, PEOPLE SKILLS AND NETWORKING

Build better relationships with everyone you know. Be genuinely interested in other people. Discover their wants and needs. From your barber to your neighbors, potential customers and unexpected paths to success exist everywhere. Develop the habit of active listening. Discipline yourself to become interested rather than interesting. Find out what people want and ask, "How can I help you get what you want?"

This is all part of building a community of like-minded associates that will support you and help you achieve success. Search for people with a strong *center of influence* and get to know them. People like this know tons of people themselves. Connecting with them will expand your sphere of influence as well. If you can provide a good service to one person, then that means potential positive feedback to other people. The key to building solid relationships like this is to understand and help other people accomplish their wants and needs. "Givers Gain®" is the philosophy and founding principal of BNI®.

BNI®, Business Network International, was founded and established in 1985 by Dr. Ivan Misner. Based in Southern California, it is a professional networking organization comprised of approximately 150,000 independent business owners worldwide who are committed to "Changing the Way the World Does Business®."

Renee and I have been members of BNI® since 2008. In 2007, Renee became a health coach with a comprehensive health system. She created a new business, Harvest Wellness. The first year, her new home-based business produced an income of $22,000. In March of 2008, Renee joined a local BNI® chapter. In 2008, the business's income more than doubled. We attribute 100% credit to Renee's membership and participation with BNI® for the doubling of her Harvest Wellness business's income.

Professional networking, and learning business marketing skills and acumen are essential to building a successful business with sustainable income. In my opinion, BNI® is the best professional networking business platform to offer this type of business education.

G.A.I.N.S.® is an educational tool developed and taught by BNI®. It is an acronym which stands for Goals, Accomplishments, Interests, Networks and Skills. Each letter denotes a topic of conversation that you can use to discover the person you are getting to know. Understanding what kind of person they are gives insight as to how you can work together towards a mutual advantage.

Discovering someone's goals and accomplishments reveals who they are by knowing what they have done and what they plan to do. Talking about one's interests is a great way to find common ground. Finding a topic that you both agree on or can at least hold a stimulating conversation about will strengthen the ties of a potential relationship.

The final letters of the acronym are more in depth in the sense they reveal what the person can do as well as for whom that do it. Finding out a person's network is another opportunity for common ground and mutual acquaintances. Also, it is a great way to expand your own sphere of influence. If a potential client is impressed with you and currently does not need your services, this is an opportunity to develop a better relationship and business by obtaining a referral a new customer. Finding out what skills they possess will assist in the long run with relationships and business development. There are limitless opportunities by building and maintaining good relationships.

Through G.A.I.N.S.® you will discover the goals and accomplishments of your own and begin to develop a stronger sphere of influence. You will discover what the types of clients and associates you enjoy working with. You will learn and develop your best skills, and understand which ones interest you most. Create ideas that are most pleasing and naturally use them to build a profitable and dynamic business.

Expanding your community is just as much about maintaining current relationships as it is establishing new ones. Statistically most people know or have access, or has access to, at least 250 names of friends or acquaintances. Search your address book or your Facebook and make a list of 100 or more people you know that could help you build success—and for whom you could do the same. Call and invite them to coffee, or meet for breakfast. Be willing to meet them at their office or invite them into your home. Find out who they are and what they want them. Understand how these goals work in conjunction with your goals.

Susan Goodsell is an Executive Director of BNI based in Southern California. She has become a friend and trusted advisor. Susan says,

"Lloyd's clear break down of the 4 Keys to Making Money really resonated with me. I'm Susan Goodsell, franchise-owner and Executive Director of BNI Riverside and San Bernardino Counties, California. As a business referral marketing professional, his recommendation of "aligning with a community of like-minded people" is the keystone of my business. And actually, that Key ties into the next two: — Establishing Better Relationships and Discovering New Possibilities — and even the first — Time Management.

Allow me to expand on the concept of referral networking for a moment. As a salesperson, you could make 35 cold calls this week. How much time is involved? More importantly, what is the success rate of turning even one of those calls into closed business? Slim to none.

Now imagine you block just ninety minutes of time weekly, to meet with thirty-five business professionals. The goal is not to sell to them, but to educate them about your business. You share a very specific aspect of your business and educate them about who you are, what you do, what you're looking for, how to listen for a need for your products and services, and how to efficiently and easily bring you up in conversations.

You then conclude with a very specific ask — a personal introduction, for example. Additionally, you consciously and systematically develop strong ties to these business professionals, building trust. Now you are leveraging your time, and strengthening relationships with a community of like-minded people. New possibilities arise which were formerly not even on your radar screen. This is BNI. Networking works.

Lloyd does not just talk theory, he walks the walk. He is a founding member, and was the first President, of BNI Wine Country Business Growers, a dynamic group of professionals in the Temecula Valley who, in a very short period of time, have become the leading chapter in our two-county region of BNI. Last year alone, Lloyd and his trusted chapter members passed more than 700 referrals to one another resulting in closed business of about $373,000 for its members! His assessment of the importance of professional business networking comes from actual results based on his experience, professionalism, and clear understanding that you can succeed in business by systematically developing strategic professional relationships. I am honored to know Lloyd and am inspired by his Givers Gain® attitude."

To learn more about a BNI® chapter in your community go to www.BNI.com.

TAKE THE NEXT STEP

Begin with a blank piece of paper. This exercise is known as "Pen to Pad." It is very useful as a creative tool. In a quiet place, take an hour or so to write out your wants, desires, dreams and interests. BE VERY CREATIVE! Just begin writing everything that comes to mind. Make a list of all the people you know as they come to mind.

Then begin to outline what you would like to accomplish over the next five years. Address what your life looks and feels like if you do not accomplish these wants and achievements. Will you have what you want, be who you want to be? If not, how will this affect you and your loved ones?

If changes are not made today to create what you want, when will you begin? Please stay away from the "Someday, I'll 'Club'" Do the steps now. You are the only one who controls your life. Do not fall into the "excuse trap." My mentor and friend Dan Bell says the definition of an excuses is a thinly veiled piece of truth, stuffed with a lie. OUCH!!! Many times in my fifty-five years I've fallen into the "excuses pit." It's an ugly and non-productive place to be.

Assess your "Pen to Pad" outline. Use the Structural Tension Tool/Chart we used in creating and purchasing your ideal home. Identify your Current Reality Baseline, list your ideas and ideals at the top as the Desired Outcome and begin to fill in between with the Action Steps on assigned Timelines. This process can take a day, days or weeks. Be assured, as you daily examine your Current Reality Baseline and keep focus on your Desired Outcome, the Actions Steps and Timelines.

Networking

Incorporate networking into your business strategy. Networking is often mistakenly viewed as a passive action, which can feel like a waste of time and money. But successful networking goes far beyond showing up to a meeting. It is proactive. It requires time and money to actively pursue it. True business networking is a way to leverage business and personal connections to bring in a regular supply of business. Great networkers do not need to do much selling because people come to them already prepared to buy.

There are many networking strategies that elite networkers utilize. They have written, long-term goals for network marketing and a strong team of referral partners. Strong networkers collaborate with a diverse personal network, which also bolsters their own skills. They research who can get them into their target market. They offer value to others, which encourages others to help them.

As a networker, you should volunteer to work on something meaningful in your community. Become an active member of your Chamber of Commerce. Host events for people in your network. Send notes and thank you cards to let people know you appreciate their relationship. Become comfortable speaking in public and ask for referrals. When you get a referral, follow up within 24 hours and ask for feedback on how you can improve. Capitalize on your hobbies and use them to meet like-minded people. Tailor your skills to provide benefits for your customers.

Do these things and your base of relationships will expand, which will build up your community in turn. As your community grows and evolves, new opportunities will develop. Fresh possibilities will emerge.

Whether you are unemployed, struggling with your business, looking for a new business, or reinventing the one you already own, the way to make more money is by meeting people that can help you create opportunities. Just remember: Be a giver. Become great at asking the question, "How can I help you?" and look for ways to help others before helping yourself. If you follow this Golden Rule, your needs will be taken care of.

Summary

Earning the supplemental income to pay off your home in five years is about knowing what you have to offer. Do the simplest thing possible. Make a list of the skills you possess and the goals you want to reach. Consolidating the two, draft a list of what products and services you could offer based on what you enjoy and what you are good at. From there, recall your favorite clients and customers or the last ten people who took advantage of your services. Ask yourself where they came from. Were they referred? Who referred them? Finding out who your best clients are and where they came from will allow you to understand how to duplicate that service with other clients.

Furthermore, this will help you establish your most profitable contact spheres. A contact sphere is your ideal circle of influence, meaning those who influence your business and those whose business is influenced by you. If you are a book writer you will want to associate with other book writers, publishers, editors, librarians, and the like. As a Realtor®, my ideal top contact spheres are CPAs, financial advisors, family and estate attorneys and other Realtors®. My goal is to be referred to those professionals and their clients and offer my real estate expertise and service.

Just as G.A.I.N.S.® helps you develop clarity about you and your associates, this process will help you begin to develop a clarity about your career and business. This will help you achieve the income you need to pay off your home in the desired amount of time. Keep working to carve out a thriving niche in the economy. Develop an enhanced community of like-minded people with strong *centers of influence.*

BUILD SIGNIFICANT RELATIONSHIPS

All this simply takes attitude and discipline. Once you have that down, you are prepared to run your own business, make a greater income and make a significant difference in your local economy.

Start now by building better relationships with the people already in your contact sphere. Improve your listening skills. Show people that you can be trusted. As you expand your own community, connect with like-minded people who share your ambition and have the resources to help you to achieve your goals. Once you begin getting to know people, you will see what they can do and how that can fit with what you do.

You can absolutely trust in yourself. Eliminate fear, doubt, and confusion. These emotions hinder good decision-making. You have the choice to educate yourself, believe in yourself, and keep your focus. Gain control of your own life. The glue that will hold your plans together is faith. If you knew with certainty you would accomplish what you set out to do, what do you believe you could do?

JAMI MCNEES STEPS OUT

Jami McNees at the age of fifty recognized she wanted to make more money and developed the courage to completely change careers. Here is a bit about Jami's career change:

"In the back of my mind I kept hearing that little voice that said, 'You're not getting any younger. You can't keep working a job that keeps you in debt. Doing the same thing is only going to get you the same results.' I knew I needed to make a change and reinvent myself, but I hate change. I love my comfort zone and all things predictable and safe. But each day, that little voice kept whispering a little louder until one day it was screaming at me. 'Jump now! Do it! Fly baby!'

What might have appeared to my friends as an impulsive jump off the career high dive for a fifty plus single woman, had actually been brewing under the surface for months. I wanted more for my life, my future retirement and for my overall peace of mind. Against the recommendation of my financial planner, I took the bold move to dip into my retirement account to sustain myself financially while I changed careers.

My financial planner wanted to "play it safe," but I was willing to risk taking five steps backward in order to move 500 steps forward. I left my position as a Payroll Service Sales Rep to reinvent my career as an Independent Insurance Agent allowing me unlimited income and potential. I used the least expensive and most flexible methods I could find to pass my licensing exams. I took courses online, ordered "used" study material from Amazon and studied like it was Final Week in college.

Passing my exams and obtaining every insurance license available allows me to sell all types of insurance. My opportunities are unlimited and I have complete peace of mind regarding my future. I'm Janci McNees — The Insurance Lady. For insurance services or just encouragement to change careers, reinventing you, you can connect with me through Lloyd's website:

www.SouthernCaliforniaRealEstateSystem.com or
www.LloydMize.com

STEVE AMANTE LEAVES COMFORTABLE CORPORATE SEAT

"Who would start a new business in 2008? Well, I did. While most people told me I was crazy, that didn't stop me. I left a position with a large insurance company to pursue my dream to own my own business. I was a Vice President of the parent company and the President & CEO of one of their subsidiary companies. Corporate life was killing my entrepreneurial spirit and the way to reignite it was to leave and build my own business. My philosophy has always been to take control of my own destiny. A common day would be 12 hours in the office and 2 to 3 hours on the freeway. Travel was also a regular practice, which I disliked immensely. Not only was my family life significantly impacted, this along with the horrible stress was affecting my health. It was clear that it was time for me to take control of my destiny and make a scary but obvious choice, regardless of the economy. I believe that a tough economy meant that you needed to work smarter, harder and longer, which I did and still do. But the long hours and hard work is for me not a large corporation. The decision to start my own business was as much for personal reasons as it was professional. I work and live in a great community. I do not waste 10 to 15% of my day on the freeway in traffic. My health improved immediately. I am able to give back to my community. While there are always tradeoffs, I look back and know that it was one of the best decisions that I have ever made."

We know, and can refer many business and/or affiliate partners that can help you with other industries you may be interested in. As an example, if you have an interest in accounting or book keeping you can create and begin a payroll service business. My good friend Mark Rowley owns and operates R&R Payroll. Here are some tips Mark offers as to how to set up your own payroll services business.

MARK ROWLEY OPENS PAYROLL BUSINESS

"I whole-heartedly agree with Lloyd's assessment of the value of a five year mortgage. In my own personal experience a five year mortgage would have been a tremendous benefit for my wife and me versus the 30 year mortgage we were dealing with in Northern California. What freedom it would have offered us to have our mortgage paid off early.

Owning a payroll service is a great way to make money. Some important steps to consider while setting up includes making sure your company secures an account with an ACH processor. This is a crucial step It gives your company the flexibility to offer direct deposit as well as tax impounds and fee collections. Cash flow is improved tremendously with the ability to collect your fees at processing time, versus paper billing and waiting to be paid.

You must also set up your company as a "bulk" taxpayer with the IRS and state tax authorities as you need to completely be on top of payroll tax payments. Timely tax payments are a key to your payroll company's success, as your client does NOT want to have to worry whether payroll taxes are paid, and paid on time.

It is similarly important to become comfortable and confident using check writing and payroll processing software. High quality payroll software can cost anywhere from $1,000 to $10,000 or more. Make sure that tax updates are part of the software package as payroll taxes are changing often these days. If your business is set up correctly, your ability to make money as a payroll processor is increased and the stress levels due to uncertainty are decreased dramatically."

INDUSTRIES, BUSINESSES, BOOKS AND MENTORS OF NOTABLE INTEREST

Before we move on to Chapter 5, "Reinventing Yourself," let's take a look at some relevant industries and businesses you may want to look into with respect to developing your own business.

An estimated one trillion dollars of wealth transference will take place over the next five years. Much of this is money changing from large public corporations to small privately-owned business. I say all the time, "There are hundreds of businesses that are easy to develop and establish as your own. Startup costs are minimal." This is an understatement! Take a minute and Google, "How many home based businesses are there in the US. In 2006, there were over two million home based businesses in the US, making up over 500 billion dollars of income. Through 2012 these numbers have come close to doubling. There has never been a better time than now to begin your own business.

Suggested industries that are hot and expanding are Real Estate, Insurance, Financial Advisory, Contracting, Health and Wellness, Beauty and Fashion and Clothing. All of these industries offer lucrative, low start-up cost and easy to establish business models.

My favorite businesses

My personal favorite industries of interest are real estate, health, wellness and fashion. Renee and I have established businesses in all three industries and we are more than happy to share with you how to get started in your business. Just get in touch through our website:

www.SouthernCaliforniaRealEstate.com or
www.LloydMize.com

MAURICE DIMINO OFFERS SPEAKING AS A BUSINESS

What is your message and passion in life? Everyone has a message to help others. The key is discovering your message. Maurice DiMino is an award winning speaker, author and mentor. He has created a business template for public speaking and delivering professional presentations and messages. Maurice has coached executives, entrepreneurs and celebrities. They have used his template and they have turned their number one fear into their number one asset.

Maurice has this to add, "If you want to make money, great! There are a large number of people making a very nice living by public speaking. I cannot think of a better time in our history than now to get more voices in the mix. Go tell the world your message!'

Maybe you are speaking in public because you need volunteers or dollars for a philanthropy you are running or organizing. I look at Public Speaking this way... You can do 100 cold calls to 100 people. Or you can gather 100 people in a room and give one warm call. I will take the latter ever time. How about you?"

Maurice DiMino, speaker, coach and author of The Sicilian Mentor.

You can connect directly to Maurice through my website, **www.LloydMize.com** or **www.SouthernCaliforniaRealEstateSystem.com**

PROPER SET UP

You can build your business quickly to make an additional $1,000 per month, and build to $30,000, $50,000 or $150,000 over two to three years. Yes, you can! It is so important your business is set up correctly, from paying yourself, accounting and taxes, and having the right legal structure. In Chapter 9, there is a list of business professionals to consult with. Fred Karma and Nicole Albrecht of Financial Accounting Services offer great accounting services. Another good business accountant is Nellie Williams, whose slogan is "Bullet Proof Your Taxes." My two favorite attorneys for business structure and real estate advice are Dale Bethel and Todd Frahm. For payroll advice as to how to set up your business for payroll my friend and business associate Mark Rowley of R&R Payroll, whom I mentioned above, is a great resource.

Chapter 5 includes my favorite books, authors and my personal top eight mentors and life coaches are listed and will help a lot to get started "reinventing yourself". Let's move to Chapter 5!

CHAPTER 5

REINVENTING YOURSELF

In this chapter, I present the idea of repositioning or reinventing yourself in three sections; emotional, physical and financial. All three begin with awareness. Before you can improve or reinvent yourself, you must acknowledge your reality. Many times in my life, I've arrived at the point of "It's just impossible and will never change or get better." What a horrible and destructive lie! No matter where you are in life, there are miracles and opportunities designed specifically for you! I promise.

Own and take personal responsibility with where you are in life and what you have created to this point. It is simple to do, as bad as it may be. Your responsibility proclamation may just begin with, "Okay, this really sucks and I'm okay with it. Now I'm ready to improve and move forward." Getting to this point is what I call a "personal ice breaker." If you practice "owning where you are" and take personal responsibility for what you have created, you will be amazed at the opportunities that will come your way and begin to unfold. But, you must be ready to recognize them and then ready to receive them.

In the previous chapters, we've talked about positioning yourself to purchase a home, accelerating the payoff to own "Free and Clear," building a business and developing wealth. Now we need to ask the obvious questions. What does a person who's made these accomplishments look like? What type of schedule do they have? How have they structured themselves? Whom do they associate with? You are really asking, "How in the heck did he or she accomplish that type of life?" When you find out, you will need to proclaim, "I want some of that!"

The point of this chapter is this: Regardless of the position you are in currently, you can always change your circumstances and be the person you want to be, achieving your most significant desires and dreams. When we say significant we are not referring to owning a hot sports car. Though it may be a motivating desire, in most circles it doesn't weigh in with significance. How does owning a sports car move the world, build better relationships, or make a better community or build health and wealth?

The pursuit of health, wealth, and happiness is significant. They make for better relationships and quality of life. Finding out how to do it is actually quite simple: Find people with a history of accomplishing what you want and are the type of people you desire to be like. Then become a master student of how they have done it. If possible, figure out how to know and associate with them. In one of my favorite mentor books, Napoleon Hill writes about a very common man, Edwin Barnes, with no assets or resource other than his God-given determination to meet and become a business partner with Thomas Edison.

He figured out a way not only to get in front of Thomas Edison, but to get hired by him. He eventually became Mr. Edison's business partner. As a result he amassed great wealth. The absolute truth is it makes no difference who you want to meet or who you are, you have the resources and ability to meet and connect with anyone you desire. Timothy Ferriss, in his brilliant book , "The Four - Hour Work-week" shares this same information about seeking/meeting/connecting with the right people. Seek out people who have what you want and are living the life you want to live. One of the greatest resources you have is people and the relationships you keep with them. Align yourself with people who have what you want. This is a big benefit of professional networking.

Start Where You Are
You may be fifty pounds beyond your desired weight. Possibly you've just declared bankruptcy, sold and settled your home in a "Short Sale" or lost it in foreclosure. You may be suffering from serious illness or just lost your significant other. Regardless of your season in life, you can decide to proclaim, position and pursue who you want to be, and possess your significant wants.

Let me return to my story for a moment. In 2007, I had just completed building my 18th home. I had successfully sold 13 of them, and kept one as a dream home for Renee and me. But we still had four other major investment properties that needed to be sold. The market had shifted overnight. Once again, I was caught with too many properties. Home prices were beginning to stall and decline. It was becoming very clear that the homes I had planned to sell in the high—$600,000 to mid—$700,000's were not going to sell at those projected prices. I settled on prices between $250,000 to $350,000 which meant selling at a loss rather than a profit. At the end of 2009, we had lost all of our cash, all of our credit, and all of our equity in real estate, including our dream home.

This failure sent me into a despair that I had not known since the death of my father in 1982. In 2009, at 52, I had lost everything for a third time in my life. Fortunately, I had built a circle of influence of associates and friends. Some were in the same situation. Some were experiencing even worse economic downturns. But others had stayed focused on their vision, followed their plan, accomplished their goals and had the freedom to sail around the world.

Some days add I felt like looking for a bridge to either live under or jump off of. What saved me was a God-given driving spirit within me, and my circle of friends and associates. I realized that this was not the end, but rather another step in the journey.

That year, in Palm Desert about 1,000 of my friends and other real estate associates gathered to hear Tony Robbins speak. Paraphrasing, I remember that he told us we are a culmination of the five people we hang around with most. So try this: Make a list of the five people you hang around with most. Find out their incomes, average them together and divide that by five. Usually the answer will be very close to your income.

Looking at the people I spent my time with most, I made the decision to seek and align with people who had what I wanted. People who possessed strong *centers of influence*. By 2009, my mantra had become: "Align with like-minded people, who have more to offer and have strong *centers of influence*."

Knowing what to do and actually putting it into action are two different things. A huge aspect of positioning yourself to purchase and own real estate Free and Clear is reinventing yourself with a certainty otherwise known as faith. Once you discover and decide your significant wants, plan and prepare with faith. Then take "effective action." When you absolutely know with certainty, you can have and accomplish your intentions, oceans part and mountains move.

People are now calling 2007 through—2009 the Great Recession. Despite that, I had determined to stabilize my $150,000 a year lifestyle. Fortunately, Renee and I had developed Harvest Wellness into a business that was bringing in over $50,000 yearly. In March 2008, I began the liquidation process, selling all my investment properties.

From there, I began selling bank-owned "R.E.O." properties, which are distressed properties that banks had foreclosed on. I was able to reinvent myself from a homebuilder and real estate investor into a local real estate R.E.O. broker in Temecula, California. I proclaimed and positioned myself as an accomplished, experienced professional Realtor® specializing in bank owned properties, known as foreclosures and short sales.

In 2009, I settled my personal residence as well as the remaining four properties as short sales to avoid foreclosure with the bank. I wanted to make it easier to re-establish my credit. By 2010, all of our credit was settled and on a rapid path to reconstruction. Cash was beginning to accumulate, my income was stabilizing, and we were getting back on track to realize our vision.

We began to experience a sense of accomplishment and certainty. We embraced those feelings, and used them to motivate us to pursue achieving our significant dreams and desires, homeownership and wealth building. Our vision and driving desire began producing results.

We also saw the benefit of the 100 pounds of weight we had lost. Our pursuit of optimal health that gave us healthy bodies and healthy minds, which helped us get through these times of stress and rebuilding. Our increased focus and energy drove home the reality that a healthy body is needed to maintain a healthy mind. Replace your bad health habits with good health habits. Apply good health to reinvent yourself to achieve. I talk more about this in the next chapter, Health and Wellness in Real Estate.

I talked earlier about the search for a bridge to either live under or jump off of, but here's the truth: The bridge is a terrible option. In 2009, as we sold and settled the investment properties, we were not in a position to purchase. But we had the opportunity to lease a property. We were very disappointed at not being able to purchase. But we knew with certainty: "We will be back!" We will be back in the purchase market, soon enough. We will never quit! We will never give up. We negotiated a two-year lease on a beautiful home with a pool home in Temecula, and spent time rebuilding our emotional lives, cash, income and credit.

Regardless of where you find yourself, know with certainty that you have God-given gifts and freedom to pursue health, wealth, and happiness. They are yours to take. Maintain your vision and keep reaching with faith and certainty.

Ask yourself: If you knew with certainty that you could accomplish all of your dreams, what would your life look like? How would that affect your family, community and your life ambitions? Think of your ideal dream for the world and your ultimate vision for your life. Then tell yourself: This is completely possible. In spite of all the ups and downs of life, your faith holds power that cannot be defeated. Remember this quote, "With faith the size of a mustard seed, you can move mountains." Napoleon Hill said, "What you can conceive in your mind and believe you can achieve." Developing a "certainty mindset" will equip you with the power to achieve anything you can conceive and believe in.

When I look back at everything I've done in my life, I can honestly say one thing: Faith and creating certainty are the two critical pieces to my success and to my ability to recover from my failures. No matter what the odds look like, or what other people say, I've found that once I discover what it is I want, and know with clarity why it is significant to me, I can accomplish anything. The same thing is absolutely true for everyone.

All humans have the potential to achieve greatness. We build giant stone and steel structures, all beginning with only a thought. We can shove energy into little balls of glass to light our rooms. We have developed the technology to connect with someone on the other side of the world in a matter of seconds. We have in us the ability to master the elements, fly to the moon and feed the starving world. Surely, we can build a thriving business, purchase a home and own it free and clear in five years. It may not be for everyone, but is available to anyone who is ready.

Let's go back to the "Pen to Pad" exercise in the last chapter. Begin writing out what you want and let your imagination run wild. Once you know what you want study the market and meet with professionals to educate yourself on what is available. When you are absolutely certain you can do something, nothing will deter your will from creating ways to make it happen.

CONTEMPORARY RESOURCES, AUTHORS, REFERENCES, BUSINESS AND LIFE COACHING

At this point I want to offer a small selection of books from my personal library. These are significant books, writers and mentors that have shaped my life of faith and certainty. Some have been referred to earlier (Chapter 9 of this book offers a more complete list.) At the very least, make the effort to Google the books, authors and coaches offered in this chapter. Start reading books about people operating from certainty and faith. This will only strengthen your own certainty and bolster your confidence.

I've categorized books into four sections. First, "Life Moving Concepts." These are the books I turn to when I'm stuck or going through a dry spell of ideas. These are good for developing interest and creating new concepts. Next, "Motivational" or what I call "Get the ball rolling and get off your butt" books. Then the "How to" books. Once you have an idea combined with motivation, you want to move to execution step as quickly as possible.

Finally, glue is required. In other words how do you keep it all together when you don't feel like it? We have all been lured in to quitting or giving up because, "YOU JUST DON'T FEEL LIKE IT." To maintain the, "Keep on keeping on" spirit and attitude, you will need self-help or life improvement books and coaching.

No one is an island! In spite of what we hear about people not needing other people, no one achieves and maintains success all by themselves. No one does it alone! We all need coaching and a hand up. Eventually and ideally, you will want to receive and maintain live personal and business coaching. So the final category is "Coaching and Self-Improvement." Nine of my top personal and business coaches are listed there.

Life Moving Concepts

- The Bible
- Think and Grow Rich—Napoleon Hill
- Blink—Malcolm Gladwell
- The Tipping Point—Malcolm Gladwell
- The New Wellness Revolution—Paul Zane Pilzer
- Good to Great—Jim Collins

Motivational and Life Building

- The Bible
- My Utmost For His Highest—Oswald Chambers
- Think and Grow Rich—Napoleon Hill
- Jesus CEO—Laurie Beth Jones
- The Richest Man in Babylon—George S. Clason
- Secrets of the Millionaire Mind—T. Harv Eker
- Who Moved My Cheese—Spencer Johnson, M. D.
- The On – Purpose Person—Kevin McCarthy
- The Miracle Morning—Hal Elrod
- Taking Life Head On—Hal Elrod

Business How To

- How to Develop Self Confidence and Influence People by Public Speaking—Dale Carnegie
- How to Stop Worrying and Start Living—Dale Carnegie
- How to Sell Network Marketing without fear, anxiety or losing your friends!—Michael Oliver
- Selling with Intention—Ursula C. Mentjes
- BNI Networking Secrets—Dr. Ivan Misner
- The 29% Solution—Dr. Ivan Misner
- Networking Like A Pro—Dr. Ivan Misner
- Master of Sales—Dr. Ivan Misner
- How Successful People Think—John C. Maxwell
- The Millionaire Real Estate Agent—Gary Keller
- The 4 – Workweek—Timothy Ferriss

Life Coaching and Self-Improvement

- The Bible
- Think and Grow Rich—Napoleon Hill
- Dr. A's Habits of Health—Dr. Wayne Scott Andersen
- Rock Star System for Success—Craig Duswalt
- The 21 Indispensable Qualities of a Leader—John Maxwell
- Your Road for Success—John C. Maxwell
- Reposition Yourself—T.D. Jakes
- The Power of Charm—Brian Tracy

- The Four Agreements—Don Miguel Ruiz
- The Miracle Morning—Hal Elrod

May I humbly suggest and offer the most significant books I've used to in my life to continually reinvent me? First the Bible: Read it like a story. With over 66 books written and compiled over centuries by more than thirty authors there are stories about human certainty that will blow you away. A great book that follows and explains the Bible is Oswald Chambers, My Utmost for His Highest. I've been a student of the Bible since 1984 and of Oswald Chambers since 1995.

For a more secular faith builder and coach, read and re-read for the rest of your life Napoleon Hill's Think and Grow Rich. This book was published in 1937 as a guide to success. Hill spent 25 years interviewing about 500 self-made millionaires. He was able to outline thirteen commonalities, philosophies, and strategies that these people lived by to achieve what they wanted. Operating from mental and spiritual certainty, these people were able to realize their ideals, build wealth and change the world for the better. Think and Grow Rich and Napoleon Hill's teaching has had a profound effect on my life of faith.

PERSONAL LIFE AND BUSINESS COACHES

As I mentioned earlier everyone needs a coach to keep them going. It is critical to renew your mind daily to be a truly transformed person. Not only do you need coaching to achieve optimal excellence in life, you need coaching to maintain consistency. It only makes sense to be excellent at what you do. Why settle for good when it is just as easy to be great? My great-grandfather Norman said, "If it's worth doing it's worth doing it with excellence." Why settle for good or just getting by? It's just as easy to be excellent as it is to be mediocre. It is much better to be excellent.

These are my top nine life and business coaches. The good news for you is that you have access to all of them! Most of them have written books, which I listed above. All are referenced and listed with additional web information in Chapter 9:

- Jesus Christ
- Oswald Chambers
- Dr. Wayne Scott Anderson
- Dr. Ivan Misner
- Mark Nicole
- Craig Duswalt
- Jim McLaughlin
- Hal Elrod
- Maryann Ehmann

TIPS FROM TOP COACHES

Jim McLaughlin
"There's nothing like the confidence that comes with having the road to success all mapped out. What you can't see, however, are the potholes and detours that can set you back.

Find the coaching that will help you deal with the challenges and keep you on the right road.

Reinventing yourself requires that you challenge long-held beliefs. You can't do that until you recognize them as 'beliefs' and not the 'truth.' These long-held beliefs have become a habitual way of being and acting for you—and you are mostly unaware of it. As a result, what you can accomplish is limited. It takes a tremendous amount of courage to reinvent yourself. You have a lot vested in the 'self' that you created."

Mark Nicole

The practice and pursuit of mastering and reinventing one's self is Mark Nicole's passion. Mark shares that their are three components that we MUST address/master in order to achieve any goals that require us to be/act/think in a way that is more than who we are today.

History: How you became who you are and understanding the unique way in which you are wired.

Present: Learn to functionally use your mind and emotions as tools in the moment to aid you in achieving your goal. This includes being clear about what seduces you to go off-track and being clear about your intended destination, and the choices you need to make to get there. It is our thoughts and emotions that drive our choices and actions. They, in turn, create our results/desired outcomes. So, if we can become masters of the internal game, then we can become masters of the external game...the game of creation, manifestation and achievement.

COMPELLING WHY

Not just a clear WHAT but an emotionally infused and intrinsically motivated WHY. Plenty of people know what they want and are fairly clear about what they need to do to get there. A lack of "how to" is not their issue or challenge.

Without having a strong connection to your greater "why," you won't make it through the challenges that are naturally generated by goals that force us to grow. We will be faced with either addressing our "stuff" and grow or give up what we say we want, remain the same and continue to get the same results that we were getting before the idea of going for the goal came to us."

Hal Elrod

"Lloyd asked me to share a little bit with you about professional coaching, and how crucial it can be to take your success/income to the next level. As someone who has both experienced the transformative benefits of working with multiple coaches over the years, as well as being a Life and Business Success Coach myself, and having now provided coaching for well over 1,000 individuals, I believe I can give you a valuable perspective to see if coaching is right for you.

Most highly successful people (world class athletes, CEOs, entrepreneurs, business owners, salespeople, etc.) consistently invest a portion of their income back into their personal and professional development, often incorporating some form of coaching. While a high level coach isn't cheap (anywhere from

$500/month to $5,000/month and more), the benefits far outweigh the cost. One of my primary focuses with my clients is almost always increasing their income, many times over what they're investing in coaching, so that the ROI, return on investment, makes hiring me a no-brainer. For example, I worked with Robert a few years ago, and I coached him on how to increase his sales by 300% in our first month of coaching, which he did. It resulted in him earning an additional $15,000 in income, which more than paid for his entire years' worth of coaching (in his first month). In summary, hiring a coach is about investing in yourself and gaining access to heightened levels of clarity, effective strategies, and systematic accountability to take yourself, and your results to levels beyond what you have ever accomplished before."

Maryann Ehmann

What Stands in the Way of Your Magnificent Life? The quest for freedom, fulfillment, and a magnificent life is built into every human being by the Creator Himself. We are born to excel, walk in greatness, and live an exceedingly abundant life! While this may seem impossible for most, with God all things are possible!

And yet...this truth, as inspiring as it sounds, is often nothing more than a platitude to us which creates frustration, guilt, and increased doubt. We ask, "Am I doing something wrong? Am I not enough? What am I not getting? Don't I have enough faith?"

Well, after asking myself these questions for years, and hearing them voiced over and over by my clients, I sought God in all sincerity for some answers. How do we manifest this magnificent life for which He created us? How do we get the results we are looking for?

And one morning, as plain as day, there it is was: *Our results will always be determined by the actions we take, but they are determined by the quality of the feelings we have, and they are triggered by the thoughts we think, which are rooted in the beliefs,* **conscious or subconscious,** *we have acquired.* **It All Starts With Our Beliefs.**

Here's a caveat, though…you can have competing beliefs! This is called double-mindedness, which is also called DOUBT.

Here's an example of what I mean: My coaching programs and speaking engagements almost always include teaching about the Favor of God and man. This is a gift available to all and we need it to accomplish the things in life God has called us to. But competing beliefs like, "I am not worthy, special, or qualified" will compete with this truth and create doubt, making it difficult for us to see and expect the favor God has for us. (As you read this, you may even be triggered hearing the word "expect.") This will make our thoughts conflicted and confused, we may feel unstable and even discouraged, and it will dilute our actions, thus giving us less than effective results.

To sum up, if your life is not reflecting the magnificent life for which you were created, follow the trail back to your beliefs and see if there are competing beliefs within. Doubt is your enemy! You are destined for greatness and to lead a fully alive life! If you would like help with this, feel free to contact me. Uncovering and transforming your mindset in partnership with the Spirit of God to help you attain a magnificent life is what I do!"

You can connect directly to Maryann and other life coaches through my website:

www.LloydMize.com or
www.SouthernCaliforniaRealEstateSystem.com.

As we wrap up our chapter on repositioning or reinventing yourself, I've asked my wife, Renee, and two very close friends and business associates, Randy Gray and Sean McHenry to share personal insights they've discovered as they have repositioned their careers at "mid-life stages".

RENEE MIZE REINVENTS AT 55

"I've always believed if you do what you love, the money will follow. Well, what I love to do is shop! How do you make money doing that? So for 30 years I've done things I didn't really love. Although I was a successful escrow officer for 20 years and have been a successful health coach for the last 6 years, I can honestly say, I didn't love either.

So, how crummy is that—55 years old and still trying to figure out what I want to be when I grow up. When Lloyd started talking about writing his book it got me to thinking. I needed a different mindset. I set out to honestly assess what I wanted to do and through that process realized, how fortunate am I? To be 55 and be able to do whatever I want! I am an Independent

Style Consultant with J. Hilburn, Men's Clothier and the largest seller of men's custom shirts in the world. Men don't necessarily like to shop so it's perfect for me. I save them time and money while shopping for their professional, social and casual wardrobes. Yes, I shop for a living and absolutely love it. I do still maintain a fair amount of health clients (some of them are even dressing better) and the Income I make is helping us to achieve the American Dream and be happy doing it."

Randy Gray, President Best Life Solutions

"Everybody dreams of 'being somebody' but most of us never get the opportunity, for various reasons, to see who we can really be. In 2007, I started a home based business. It has given me the option to build my life around what matters most to me. For example, options of being able to leave a very good job and to relocate to another state to be close to family as they get older because it was important to us.

Building your life around what matters most to you may lead you to discover that you can become the biggest somebody you can be to those that are most important to you. The suggestions and steps Lloyd gives in this book are time tested and work. They worked well for us as we've developed new business opportunities and now we have the flexibility to live where we choose."

Sean McHenry, Insurance and Financial Services Specialist

"On December 23, 2007, my world changed with the birth of my son Riley Patrick McHenry. But on January 5th, 2010, there were events that would reshape my life.

I was part of one the most successful golf car dealerships in Southern California and nationally recognized with numerous awards. The business was sold to a competitor. Within in few months, the new owners had changed our business model so much that the business failed and I was out of a job.

I had to reinvent myself. Right around that time, a friend who sat in front of us at a Charger game started telling me about her new career as an Aflac agent, to which I scoffed that I wasn't an insurance guy. But she was persistent and eventually I had a two hour discussion with some of their executives that ultimately changed my course.

My new business is now evolving as a solid provider of supplemental and voluntary medical insurances along with life insurance, annuities, financial services, and benefits for US Senior Veterans. I truly believe that 2013 and beyond, our business will explode as medical reform starts to take shape.

In addition, I've partnered with Lloyd and others to build and establish the strongest BNI chapter in the Riverside/San Bernardino counties. We refer to and think of our business network as an economy within an economy. Our BNI region in 2012, referred and closed over ten million dollars in fees and services."

KNOW WITH CERTAINTY

Know that you can achieve everything if you have certainty. Simply proclaim who you are and be certain of what you want. Be very careful with your thoughts, words and proclamations. If you have faith in yourself, nothing can deter your ambition. Once you acquire faith and certainty, people won't be able to deter your will or damage your ego and pride. If you are certain in your endeavors, you will have the drive to realize your dreams. Be certain in all you do. It will strengthen and empower you to carry out your plan to not only purchase and own your own home free and clear in five years, but also pursue and obtain health, wealth and happiness.

REINVENTING GREAT CREDIT AND FINANCIAL SOLVENCY

Finally, let's address how you can go from horrible credit to perfect credit, and from insolvency to financial greatness. Again, it's quite simple—just follow the steps. In many cases credit can be restored in six months up to two years, or three years if you have foreclosures to deal with.

Tiffany Hazelaar—Dedicated Credit Repair

"Ultimately Dedicated Credit Repair understands that trusting a company with your credit is not an easy thing to do. That's why we treat every credit file as if it were our own. You will find the walls of our office lined with recent testimonials from lenders, Realtors® and past clients who have raved about our services.

We can help clients in all FICO Score ranges. Lower FICO scores can be boosted by a score of 60-90 points in a time frame of three to six months, when all the required steps are followed. We provide consultations as well as client status reports via phone, webinar or Skype to accommodate our clients all over the U.S.

In every industry, there are the "Good Guys" and the "Bad Guys". In the credit repair industry there are far more people operating without integrity than those doing things the right way. That is why Dedicated Credit Repair is such an incredibly valuable resource to lenders, Realtors® and clients who have a hunger for accurate credit advice and quality credit repair. When consumers have to face the hard decision of whether or not to short-sale their home, file bankruptcy, or settle collection debt it is imperative that they seek counsel from a company who can give them accurate guidance.

Please connect with Dedicated Credit Services through Lloyd's website:

www.SouthernCaliforniaRealEstateSystem.com or
www.LloydMize.com. We look forward
to hearing from you.

CHAPTER 6

HEALTH AND WELLNESS IN REAL ESTATE

What if you could have Health, Wealth and happiness; your ideal body, look and feel; your dream home owned "Free and clear" and happiness in spite of all the challenges of life? You are in control. You have the ability to own and have all you desire. Just follow the simple strategies that I am laying out for you. Not everyone is ready for them, but they apply to anyone who is ready to take action. The strategies are time tested, proven, simple and easy to follow. That includes the health and wellness strategies I'm about to show you.

What does health and wellness have to do with purchasing and owning real estate? That's a good question—and I have an even better answer. If you are not healthy, you won't feel well. You probably won't look well. If you do not feel well, your ability to make good decisions is limited. Your motivation to pursue what is important to you and your family will be lacking. The desire to give up will be knocking at your door all the time.

Acquiring great health and wellness is the key to a long and successful life. Renee and I discovered a healthy body leads to a healthy mind. A healthy mind leads to healthy finances. (As a side note, because of healthy life style choices Renee and I look and feel great!) What if you could have the body and health you have always wanted? How would this affect your decisions, moods and attitude about life and other people?

Remember in May of 2007, when the market drastically shifted, I was 40 pounds overweight and Renee was about 60 pounds overweight. We were exhausting ourselves on bad habits and "yo-yo" dieting. We learned that an overwhelming 85% of people that diet end up gaining their weight back in the next year. We no longer wanted to be a part of this statistic. We recognized we looked horrible. We were on Round 3 of big clothes. We did not have energy. We were not sleeping right. More significantly, at 50 years of age, we were susceptible to hearts attacks, strokes, high blood pressure, and other health issues. We recognized that change had to happen with urgency.

To "trim the fat," Renee immersed herself in health research. Over a period of six months, we found many of options. We could try "fat farms" in Canada or Texas, liquid diets, or hire a very expensive Personal Fitness Trainer that would show up to our home 3 to 4 days a week at five O'clock in the morning and beat us into healthy submission. None of these options were appealing. They all seemed like we would still have the same struggle around losing weight. After the goal was accomplished, we would eventually morph back to fat and die.

One day in May 2007, Renee found a comprehensive health system through the company mentioned previously co-founded by Dr. Andersen and his "Dr. A's Habits of Health". The system specializes in helping people achieve optimal weight by trading in unhealthy habits for healthy habits. We followed the very simple curriculum in Dr. A's Habits of Health. It has helped 100s of thousands of Americans get to their healthy weight and maintain a healthy life style. Dr. A's health system is simple and easy to follow. It all begins with eating portion-controlled meals every three hours.

After five months of sticking to the very simple plan of eating every 3 hours, I had lost fourty pounds and Renee had shed sixty as well. Furthermore, Renee got off all but one of the prescribed high blood pressure and high cholesterol medications. We not only looked fantastic, we felt better and had more energy than ever.

This was perfect timing for us, with the stress and pressures that the "Great Recession" was about to bring over the next five years. We are so thankful! We believe that our health improvements before the economic downturn enabled us to weather the next five years, and close ourselves off to the possibility of strokes and heart attacks.

It was easy. We just followed laid out rules. We looked better and felt better; we were getting more and better sleep. By developing a healthy body, we gained clear minds. Able to think more clearly, could approach situations without confusion. Our efficiency improved in our business, personal lives and our relationships changed and began to flourish.

Once we had each shed some weight, a friend noticed and asked what we were doing. We told him about the health system we had discovered. He connected directly to Dr. Andersen and learned there was a big business opportunity with Dr. Andersen's comprehensive health system. Five years prior to our wellness revelation, a book was written by Paul Zane Pilzer called The Wellness Revolution. Pilzer's book detailed the growing interest in health and wellness and the possibilities for lucrative businesses surrounding the health and wellness industry. Pilzer stresses the importance of maintaining positive health for benefits beyond physical wellness; benefits such as saving on health insurance and, to the business-minded, other financial gains.

No matter what you are trying to accomplish, you need to get healthy. With your health issues solved, you can focus on more important and long-term goals. Problems like obesity in yourself or your children, finding health care, or paying medical fees, can all be solved by simply remaining healthy.

How healthy are you? There are many methods to help you overcome illness and develop a lifestyle of optimal health. My good friend and business associate Dr. Alisha Moadab, N.D. offers this advice, "Naturopathic Medicine can be described as a path to health via a variety of natural methods, while getting to the root cause of an illness, treating the whole person, realizing prevention is the best medicine, and being true to the Latin word for doctor, docere (meaning to teach) patients how to live a healthy lifestyle. All of this, while upholding the Hippocratic oath to, first do no harm. Good health, is the ultimate key to wealth. If you don't have your health, what else can one have to fully enjoy?" —In Good Health & Beauty, Dr. Alisha Moadab, N.D.

We developed a passion for health in our lives that enables us to do anything we set our minds to. We were introduced to Dr. Andersen, and became certified as Health Coaches, to begin a home business ourselves. Through proper maintenance of our own bodies we turned our lives around and bolstered ourselves to successfully navigate the Great Recession.

It is interesting to note that as our country floundered with a changed economy, we are also statistically fatter than we have ever been. When we mention reviving the American dream, we are talking about a dream that is all-inclusive. Paying off your home in five years, property acquisition, gaining wealth, and maintaining good health may seem like daunting tasks. But with creativity, faith and certainty you can position yourself to accomplish all these things.

Creatively interrelate your goals so that by achieving one you are working towards achieving another. According to Pilzer, the wellness industry is a soon-to-be one trillion dollar industry. Currently, weight loss alone is a 65 billion dollar industry. Pursue good health for yourself, while creating a supplemental income and help do the same. As you help others, you can save money for a down payment, and cover your PITI monthly payments, even before you buy a home. This can even shorten your mortgage pay-off time.

As you pay-off your house, purchase investment property to create wealth and reduce your mortgage loan payment plan to five years or less. Once your home is paid off, purchase other investment properties and pay them off sooner rather than later until everything you own is either paid off or paying itself off. You will be self-funded and financially secure.

It begins with maintaining good health, and it will lead you to Park Place with hotels on the "Monopoly Board" of life. You will not only "Pass Go and collect $200" but you will also gain wealth every time you help someone get healthier.

You must find a health system. Dr. Andersen's "Habits of Health" system is a great system that works. It starts you off with a basic self-health assessment based on your weight and height. You can see where you currently fall and where a good place to begin may be. You can reference the chart included on this page. Or, for a more in-depth assessment, you can utilize the health assessment link found at www.HarvestWellness.com. This link provides a real, "In-your-face assessment" of just how healthy you are.

DO YOU KNOW YOUR BMI?

Body Mass Index (BMI) Table																	
	19	20	21	22	23	24	25	26	27	28	29	30	31	32	33	34	35
Height	Weight (in pounds)																
4'10" (58")	91	96	100	105	110	115	119	124	129	134	138	143	148	153	158	162	167
4'11" (59")	94	99	104	109	114	119	124	128	133	138	143	148	153	158	163	168	173
5' (60")	97	102	107	112	118	123	128	133	138	143	148	153	158	163	168	174	179
5'1" (61")	100	106	111	116	122	127	132	137	143	148	153	158	164	169	174	180	185
5'2" (62")	104	109	115	120	126	131	136	142	147	153	158	164	169	175	180	186	191
5'3" (63")	107	113	118	124	130	135	141	146	152	158	163	169	175	180	186	191	197
5'4" (64")	110	116	122	128	134	140	145	151	157	163	169	174	180	186	192	197	204
5'5" (65")	114	120	126	132	138	144	150	156	162	168	174	180	186	192	198	204	210
5'6" (66")	118	124	130	136	142	148	155	161	167	173	179	186	192	198	204	210	216
5'7" (67")	121	127	134	140	146	153	159	166	172	178	185	191	198	204	211	217	223
5'8" (68")	125	131	138	144	151	158	164	171	177	184	190	197	203	210	216	223	230
5'9" (69")	128	135	142	149	155	162	169	176	182	189	196	203	209	216	223	230	236
5'10" (70")	132	139	146	153	160	167	174	181	188	195	202	209	216	222	229	236	243
5'11" (71")	136	143	150	157	165	172	179	186	193	200	208	215	222	229	236	243	250
6' (72")	140	147	154	162	169	177	184	191	199	206	213	221	228	235	242	250	258
6'1" (73")	144	151	159	166	174	182	189	197	204	212	219	227	235	242	250	258	265
6'2" (74")	148	155	163	171	179	186	194	202	210	218	225	233	241	249	256	264	272
6'3" (75")	152	160	168	176	184	192	200	208	216	224	232	240	248	256	264	272	279

Most people consider themselves to be in good health when they are not sick. Find out how healthy you really are and check out great options for achieving your optimal health by going to Renee's Harvest Wellness website: www.HarvestWellness.com.

Dr. Andersen has become a significant mentor and friend to Renee and me. He offers this to every one:

"Did you know that ours is the first generation whose quality of life is actually less than that of our parents? It's a fact: Our technologically advanced society is no longer serving our best interests. America is critically unhealthy by being overweight. Obesity is at an alarming all-time high. I've dedicated my life and resources to "Get America Healthy." I would like to encourage you to take advantage of the resources in my book, "Dr. A's Habits of Health." Begin by taking a look at Renee's website, www.HarvestWellness.com. Take time and begin the journey of achieving a healthy life style one simple step at a time. Lloyd and Renee have become personal friends and reliable business associates. From 2007 forward they've adopted and continue to pursue a healthy life style, Renee has helped hundreds of friends and clients to develop healthy habits resulting in a longer healthier life It truly is a journey, please join us and let's get America healthy."

—Dr. Wayne Scott Andersen

Did you know in 1960, that the average American would only consume 1,980 calories a day? By 2009, the statistical average caloric intake was 3,700 per day. We are increasing our unhealthy habits exponentially, but we can stop! We can make money, get happy, and become successful doing it. In Dr. Andersen's *Habits of health*, he speaks of having fulfillment and achieving success. He talks about structural tension from a medical viewpoint. He coaches the way to our Desired Outcome from our Reality Base.

I adapted my model for structural tension in real estate from him. Begin by asking the questions of what you want. Follow up with the question of why do you want it? Then, build your primary choices around what you want. What do you want? I want to maintain good health, eat well and follow a health system. If you want a cheeseburger with fries and a shake, assess if this is a choice that supports your primary goal.

Align your choices with your primary goals. If you really want a house you need to have a compelling why that will push you to achieve it. Make the best choices and discard the ones that will not achieve your primary goal. Remember: You are in control! If you want to lease a sports car for $600 a month, you can do it. However, $600 a month can be applied to your primary goal of paying off your home in five years and achieving wealth. Maintaining a healthy body bolsters positive, beneficial, and lucrative decision-making. The key to having a healthy mind lies with the discipline of maintaining a healthy body.

Make it a daily mental exercise to keep your decisions and choices aligned with what you really want. This phrase has helped me a lot: "Stop, challenge myself and then choose exactly to do what will get me what I want."

When you are trying to lose weight and a tasty off-diet meal becomes an option, stop before you decide to eat it. Challenge the decision in your own mind. Decide if the secondary decision of splurging on some food is aligned with your primary decision of maintaining good health. Or if you want to buy a new car, ask if this decision is aligned with paying off your home in five years. The equivalent of a sports car payment can literally take off fifteen years of mortgage payments based on a $300,000 mortgage.

You can choose to have optimal health. Line up your choices with your primary goals. Understand that you are in control of every decision you make. Figure out what you want and why you want it, and establish how you see yourself. Ask yourself if who you are now will get you what you want. Like the structural tension rubber band, if you do not see yourself as someone that can get what you want, then make the change to become a person that can achieve your desired outcome. You are in control of the outcome of your health, wealth and happiness.

Gina is one the best health coaches that I have ever worked with. Her knowledge and expertise in her field has made a difference in many lives.

"Every day, I have the privilege of working with people who have made the fundamental choice to create health in their lives. Where once it was about "fatness," the transformation that happens in a person when it becomes about health is absolutely revolutionary. I never tire of celebrating the better energy, creativity, productivity, relationships and clarity that my clients' reports week after week as they regain their health and take back their lives. And when people take back their lives, hope springs forth and anything is possible! It's awesome." — Gina Reinecke, Certified Health Coach

Live healthy and maintain a sharp mind. You will position yourself to be successful in your goals of home ownership and financial freedom.

CHAPTER 7

PURCHASING INVESTMENT PROPERTY

In the previous chapters, I have laid a solid foundation as you begin the journey to purchase your home and own it "Free and clear" in five years. Now let's move on to other real estate investments. At this point, let's assume you have purchased your home and are financially stable. Now begin to set your mind on long-term strategies to build wealth and reduce your home mortgage payment plan to five years.

Purchasing investment property is a strategic way to generate wealth beyond your business or other income. The number one reason to purchase investment property is to build wealth and sustainable income. Real estate is a tangible asset which can generate income for itself. Real estate as an asset also has the ability to appreciate in value, as well as bring in monthly income.

The three types of real estate investments include: Residential property (both single family residences and multiple family residences), commercial and industrial property and real estate investment trusts, also known as REITs.

Residential properties include single-family residences, generally referred to as SFRs, apartment spaces, and condominiums. Commercial properties are office buildings, retail buildings, and industrial buildings. A REIT or Real Estate Investment Trust is a real estate syndication or company that offers shares of investments, which provide ownership to real estate investments and delegates the management of the properties to professional investors.

For the purposes of this chapter we will use residential SFR properties as an example. Residential property is a wise investment for a great reason: Everyone needs a place to live, and always will.

There are other types of investments a property investor can make. Flipping property is a way to make quick money as I did with my Surfside beach condo in 1984. However, we are speaking in terms of generating wealth beyond the $200 at "Go." Therefore, we are talking about long-term investments, which you can purchase and hold to create sustainable income. Flipping property, in my view, is only for the experienced. To gain the experience, partner with a "Professional Flipper" until you can confidentially proclaim, "I can do this and make a profit." There are lots of hidden elements that can go wrong, quickly.

Flipping Properties

James Brennan is owner and general manager of Pacific Coast Realty Group, PCRG, based in Southern California. I am the corporate real estate broker for PCRG. From 2010 through 2012 James successfully and masterfully negotiated, purchased and flipped dozens of homes in Southern California. He is truly the best I've ever worked with. Many flippers in 2010 – 2012 thought they were going to make easy money in 90 to 120 days, but ended up losing their shirts.

James offers this advice: "Flipping is a compelling and attractive way to make fantastic, short term money in real estate. However it requires a thorough education in the specific market you are looking to purchase and flip in. It also requires the resources and professional knowledge of how to restore and reconstruct a property. You have got to know with absolute accuracy what your costs are to restore, market and sell the prospective property in order to make a reasonable profit."

"If you cannot confidently know your margins, profit and time frame with a ninety day exit-strategy, stay away from flipping by yourself and work with a professional until you gain the knowledge and expertise to be confident and profitable on your own. Lloyd and I are on the same page with home ownership and real estate investments. Real estate is the best wealth builder. But it does require following time tested and proven steps and does take discipline and knowledge. You can trust the steps and advice that Lloyd has laid out in his book.

Yes, work at paying off all of your real estate sooner than later. You can pay off your home in five years! Educate yourself and follow the steps with discipline."

Invest and Hold

Of the three basic categories mentioned above let's key in on SFRs to use as our investment modul. Like the other categories, a SFR can be purchased and rented out to generate enough income to pay itself off. The first step in purchasing real estate is to secure free and clear home ownership. Once your home is established with a plan in place to pay it off sooner than later then begin to plan and pursue investment properties.

Purchasing investment property is different from homeownership; however, the principles are similar. You still need to educate yourself on the market and know what you are looking for. Additionally, always remember to avoid over-leveraging. This was one of my big mistakes when I purchased Temecula investment property. Over-leveraging means owning property with too much debt.

It is very easy to purchase property with debt and quickly become financially insolvent when the market turns in a less favorable direction. A safe guideline to follow is to have at least 20% down payment when purchasing investment property. Keeping a policy of a 20% down payment creates a simple check and balance. With a 20% down payment, the monthly rent should not only cover the full PITI mortgage payment but also cover one to two months of unexpected vacancy, monthly maintenance for the property and professional property management fees.

The purpose of an investment property is to generate wealth and to do that the rent needs to at least cover its own mortgage payments. Doing so, the rent over thirty years, will completely payoff the mortgage. Now, apply the mindset of owning the investment property "Free and clear" sooner rather than later. Once the mortgage is completely paid off, the investment property begins creating long-term, sustainable income.

Using the example of a SFR in the $200,000 price range, with 20% down payment the PITI payment will total to about $1,068. This is based on a 4.5% interest rate amortized over thirty years. This breaks down to a principal and interest payment of $810 a month. Add another $208 for property taxes. Property insurance adds approximately $50. This all adds up to a monthly PITI payment of approximately $1,068. At a minimum you want to at least break even based on the fair market rent collected.

Investment property is bought with the goal of generating of positive cash flow. Ultimately, you want to keep the rent all for yourself. You need the mortgage paid off to accomplish this. That can be done with the tenant's monthly rent. You also need the rent to cover three other expenses: Maintenance, vacancy coverage and professional property management. Typically, you should set the rent 15% higher than the PITI to cover maintenance costs. Add an additional 10% of your base mortgage payment to cover an unexpected vacancy. A reasonable monthly property management fee is $125. Ideally, the base rent your charge needs to cover these cost.

Look for investment property that fits the model of a 20% down payment in a market where you can charge enough rent to cover the PITI, maintenance, vacancy and management fees. This simple guideline will ensure the property pays for itself. This combined with the mindset of "Free and clear own ability sooner rather than later is a winning combination for wealth development. In a nutshell, this simple investment strategy will build a portfolio of appreciating assets offering long term sustainable income.

In down markets in 1980, 1989-1994, and 2007-2009, I had to liquidate all my properties. I made the mistake of purchasing too many properties at one time with very little down payment. Unable to obtain market rents that would sustain the monthly expense, I had to painfully sell all the properties.

This is a basic overview of purchasing investment properties. Many books have been written on commercial properties, quick investment properties, and aspects of residential property investments like condominiums and apartments. To wrap it up, follow this simple formula and work with real estate professionals that you can trust and that you like. Ask to see references and resumes of their experiences and accomplishments.

About Property Management

Catherine Perrotta is the owner and general manager of DP Properties. She offers this insight and advice regarding property management.

"If you are not a professional property manager, you could find yourself in over your head. Collecting rent may sound easy, but in reality, it can be tedious and exhausting. If you are not familiar with rent collection, you can quickly find that your residents are taking advantage of you. In addition to rent collection, day-to-day maintenance of a rental property can be tiring. If you are not operating your property as a full-time job, you may not have the time to address tenant concerns and repairs in a timely manner. This may make hiring a property management company an excellent choice. Hiring a property management company should result in more free time and less worry for you.

Our management team is one of the best in the industry, having over thirteen years of experience in property management, as well as boasting two awards for Property Manager of the Year in San Diego and Riverside County to Budgeting awards and Community appeal awards. From our office staff to our vendors we are committed to providing excellence.

My advice is to begin with your home. Come up with a strategy to own it over five years by creating additional income. Begin educating yourself as to where the better real estate investments are, and start purchasing investment property."

Infomercials and quick-buck agents will sell the idea of buying a home without credit, income, or a down payment. This fails as a healthy, wealth building plan. Paying off your home gives you financial freedom. Purchasing investment properties and charging rent to generate a self-stimulating cash flow creates sustainable long term income and generates woalth.

What if you purchased two investment properties a year over ten years, and paid them all off over a total of fifteen years? At the end of fifteen years, your long term sustainable income could be as much as $254,400 annually. This does not take into account the property values or annual appreciation of the property income over time.

I caught up with my good friends mentioned earlier, Miguel and Lupita Castillo, as they are sailing around the world. They have successfully followed this plan. When I interviewed them in Panama, they weighed in with the following:

> "Purchasing real estate for long term investment and retirement income strategy is easy if you follow the steps Lloyd offers in his book. Lupita and I met Lloyd way back in 1984 and together began talking big stories about buying real estate as a means to build wealth. By the end of 1989, Lupita and I had purchased several properties. Into the 1990s, several more were purchased. At that point, we refinanced all of our properties and placed them in mortgages to have them paid off in fifteen years or sooner. By 2005, we were all "Free and clear," as Lloyd likes to say, and our

retirement was fully funded. We believe and now see we could have accomplished all of this sooner but for us fifteen years was a remarkable achievement.

Set a goal of buying one house every three years. In fifteen years you will have accumulated five houses. If you can afford fifteen year fixed rate loans, the first home will be paid off when you are buying your fifth. Use the positive cash flow from the free and clear homo to accelerate pay-off of house number two. You should be able to pay of all homes in the subsequent five years leaving you with five free and clear homes in twenty years.

Other considerations when investing in residential real estate are of course:

- Location: Stay in a desirable rental neighborhood with historically low vacancy rates.

- Cash flow: Try to achieve a break even or positive cash flow if possible. A small negative cash flow is acceptable as rents will rise over time and if you obtain a fixed rate loan your payments will remain almost level.

- Age and condition: Buy a newer or better maintained home, or have the cash and plan in place to restore the home.

- Tenants: The importance of good tenant screening cannot be under estimated. You will become their largest creditor. Pre-screen for credit, income, assets and rental and work histories. Hold out for the best candidates.

- Service: You are a service provider. Keep your tenants happy by responding to their needs and making timely repairs and improvements. This will minimize vacancies and turnovers. If you don't want to do this, hire a competent property manager.

- Financial freedom and Independence

- Diversification strategy: Produce passive income diversifying in three categories, Real Estate, Stocks and Bonds, and Cash.

- Psychological discipline.

- Income earning years set a percentage of monthly income in savings.

- Be an investor instead of a consumer.

- Live with goals daily, monthly and annually.

- Plan and live with a set budget daily, monthly and annually. Stick to it!

- Cut spending wherever you can.

- Review all insurance coverages when they come due. Examine higher deductibles to cut costs.

- When flush with money, save more. When times are tough, pull in the belt.

Investing Outside of Real Estate

As Mr. and Mrs. Castillo suggest it is important to have a "well rounded" investment strategy and plan in place. This does include more than real estate. I would like you to meet John Dubots. John is a trusted financial advisor, business associate and friend. He has a few tips and ideas to share.

John is President and Founder of Capital Management and has been working in the financial services industry helping his clients build, preserve and distribute wealth since 1991. He is an Investment Advisor, with multiple securities and insurance licenses. He attended the University of New Hampshire and received a B.S. in Resource Economics and a Masters in Public Administration.

John says, "To use an analogy of what I do for people I help them to build their Dream Home. You truly are the architects of your home. You know what you want to live in someday. You have a picture in your mind. My role is that of the general contractor you would hire to make sure the best skilled laborers are hired to build your home. If there are tax issues we'll need an accountant; if there's a will or trust, we'll need an attorney. Possibly equities, bonds, life insurance, annuities and of course other real estate investments will be a part of this dream home. I agree with Lloyd and his 'Free and clear' real estate strategies. Building wealth is a mindset.

My role is to find the best people or companies for those features and bring them together to build your dream home. To do that job well, I have to get a good picture of what your dream home looks like. What kind of rooms, fixtures, windows and features does it have?

My business philosophy is simple. Every client has unique dreams, goals and objectives for their retirement. Each client faces potential challenges in the form of inflation, taxes, life changes and a fluctuating economy. At Capital Management, our primary goal is to provide asset preservation guidance, active portfolio management and to offer safe money solutions to meet your unique needs. In a plan tailored to you, we'll develop solutions to minimize risk and offer options for growth over the course of your retirement.

Financial decisions don't have to be confusing. Arming you with useful information and education helps you make informed choices and provides the roadmap you need to navigate your future."

You can contact John through our website: **www.SouthernCaliforniaRealEstateSystem.com** or **www.LloydMize.com** for a complimentary consultation to discuss your specific situation and let him help you protect and preserve your retirement savings.

Wrapping Up Investments

My outline is the basic foundation to approach purchasing investment property with wisdom and will lead the right person to become a "Donald Trump" or a "Warren Buffet". Let's move on to Chapter 8. It brings "Certainty" to the five year plan of "Free and clear" ownership living in Southern California.

REALLY, PURCHASE A HOME AND PAY IT OFF IN FIVE YEARS?

The answer to the question in this chapter's title is: "Absolutely yes—if you are ready!" My passion is to promote this message throughout Southern California. I want to encourage people to realize that they have resources within themselves to accomplish their God-given visions and passions. Inside each of us lies seeds of greatness and fantastic potential. Be encouraged to dream. Learn to be in touch with your vision by knowing what your strongest desires are. These God-given desires cannot be taken from you—they are yours to accomplish.

One of the core ideas throughout this book is the importance of getting in touch with your vision by becoming very clear about what you want. Remember, you need to align what you want with a compelling why. This will grant you certainty and bolster your faith, equipping you with the proper mindset to achieve your passions.

We talked about our country being founded on the ideals of private property ownership and noted that people have literally fought here in pursuit of this dream. Today, nothing has changed. There is absolutely no better tool to build wealth, health, and happiness than to purchase your own home/ property, and pay it off as quickly as possible. A five-year plan is absolutely achievable to everyone. It is a matter of making this your want, and backing that up with an understanding of what this will accomplish for your life. Then, you can make the correct choices that will position you to achieve the goal.

With your dream home envisioned, you can start making that home yours. Apply all the different strategies I've talked about in this book:

- Find out what your purchasing power is, and do research on the market so that you can partner with your Realtor® to get what you want.

- Take care of yourself both physically and mentally. A healthy mind is necessary to maintaining positive emotional intelligence and a healthy body bolsters a healthy mind.

- Use the Structural Tension Tool often. Chart out your Reality Base and your ideal outcome, creating action steps and a timeline.

- Exercise the creativity within you and put your creativity into action. You always have options.

- Create a business for supplemental income and increase your income by $12,000, $100,000, $150,000 and more so that you can raise your purchasing power. There are 100s of viable new businesses within relevant industries available today for you to take advantage of. Research them and discover those that interest you. With digital and social media, many more are growing daily. Pick one that aligns with your interests and passions. Learn to control your own outcome.

When you find what you want, approach the five-year plan with patience. Take time to develop an achievable plan. Work with a 30-year plan first, while you develop your business. Then, adapt the plan to achieve more in less time. Hold off on frivolous spending (like motorcycles and big motorhomes) until your home is paid off. Be patient, optimistic and stubbornly disciplined to achieve and accomplish your Desired Outcome. Once you are secure with your plan, look to other investments to take your plan down to fifteen, ten, and finally to five years.

I have been transparent with my own missteps and failures. Over-leveraging, ignoring market changes and spending too much were decisions that delayed my primary goal. Still, I live in a beautiful home in Temecula. I own thriving businesses. I am exactly where I want to be. No matter how hard or how far you fall, never give up. Reinvent yourself daily and learn the power of reassessing and reshaping your character.

Build up a quality sphere of influence, and when you do fall or make missteps, there will be a network of friends and associates to help set you back on track. As with the Surfside condo, I owe many of my initial about recoveries to the aid of partners who knew and trusted me. This is the significance of networking. If you are intentional about aligning yourself with like-minded people with strong *centers of influence*, you will have a peer group that can help you—and that you can help too. Sharpen networking as a skill. Add it to your wealth-building tool belt. Networking will bolster you and your business.

Purchase investment property. Use the rental income to pay it off sooner rather than later. Make it your own and not the bank's. When managed efficiently, investment property will pay itself off, and will ensure that your retirement plan is self-funded. Pursue a healthy body and mind to achieve optimal health, wealth, and happiness. Follow this plan and retire in good health with financial security.

I have been around the Monopoly Board a few times now and I have won "free parking," but I have also had to "go directly to jail without passing go." My mistakes are apparent, but they have also honed my skill of recovery and reinventing. Recognizing what I want and why, combined with faith, determination and continual reassessment, means that my dreams and desires are in reach.

Southern California

I am grateful to have grown up and live in Southern California. It is, in my opinion, the best place on earth to live. I would like to wrap up this chapter with my connection to Southern California and its significance.

My family relocated to Southern California in 1941. I was raised here, and embrace it as my home. Renee and I have enjoyed traveling through most of the United States. We have good friends and family scattered all over our great nation. Southern California is not just our home—it's our home of choice. I have a deep love and passion for the whole area. I enjoy the people, the politics and the opportunity to influence people and to be influenced by other Southern California residents.

We have endless networking opportunities that allow us to connect with like-minded and faith-based individuals. I believe God has blessed our region despite misdeeds and our loss of focus from time to time. Southern California is absolutely the best place to live. Take advantage of what is available.

Southern California as a region is shaped by its diversity, and the passion of hard-working citizens. We have created one of the best economies in the world. At a minimum, California's economy is between 8th and 9th in the world; every year. Some years, we are even been between 5th and 6th. Yes, we do have an out of control state government with spending and taxing issues, but government and representation can be corrected and changed with citizens becoming better educated, involved, engaged and voting.

With over 22,000,000 people, Southern California boasts the largest regional population in the country. Our nine counties: Los Angeles, Ventura, Santa Barbara, Kern, Orange, San Diego, Riverside, San Bernardino, and Imperial, are home to some of the largest cities in the country as well. There are thirty-two cities in the region have a population over 100,000 people.

We have a wonderful geography and ecosystem. Our fantastic topography allows citizens to live within driving distance to twenty one of the country's most popular theme parks, from Knott's Berry Farm and Disneyland, to Sea World and Magic Mountain. We have over fourteen major wine regions in California. In Southern California, there are fifteen National Forest and Parks. We have many thriving industries, including film and entertainment corporations, sports teams, agriculture, and tourism, as well as aerospace, automotive, construction, software, and bio-medical companies.

We host international seaports, and have thriving local businesses. Our environment is envied because of how comfortable the weather is with cool summers and lovely winters. Furthermore, our massive railway, highway, and road systems allow for such a widespread community to coexist as a unified region that includes thriving metropolises such as San Diego and Los Angeles, as well as economically flourishing suburbs like Temecula Valley.

Opportunity is available to you if you recognize it. Take advantage of your geography, community and your network.

You are in control and have everything in your power to be positioned to achieve your goals.

This book is written from thirty-five years of experience, accomplishment and my personal library's worth of acquired knowledge. Allow me to encourage my fellow Southern Californians as well as anyone else reading this to step forward and take control of your wealth, health and happiness. Pursue wealth, health and happiness, and encourage others to do the same thing. That way you will create opportunities and accomplish all that your dreams.

Chapter 9 is my wrap up and "keep in touch" chapter. It offers web links, authors, books, and recommendations to professionals that have assisted me in my journey. It also introduces my website, www.SouthernCaliforniaRealEstateSystem.com. You can also go to that site by visiting www.LloydMize.com. My site is designed to support the ideas and resources contained in this book. It also is a great way for you and me to keep in touch. Let me know how you are doing and how I can help you achieve your goals of wealth, health and happiness.

CHAPTER 9

GO TO GUIDE, LINKS, REFERENCES AND NETWORKS

Throughout the book, I have made references and recommendations. This Chapter is designed to be a "Go to Guide" for you to follow up and communicate with my references, resources and networks. Please do your own "due diligence." These are my personal and professional sources. They are not for everyone, but all have worked very well for me and others.

Also, Reviving the American Dream in Southern Californian has a corresponding web site, **www.SouthernCaliforniaRealEstateSystem.com** or **www.LloydMize.com.**

Both URLs are directed to the same site. Through my website you can communicate directly with me, blog with me and locate other tips, recourses and access my professional referral network.

My hope and passion is to engage and encourage friends, clients and associates to pursue health, wealth and happiness. As we wrap up there are a few points I want to leave with you.

First, thank you! Thank you for taking time to read my book. Purchasing a home and creating additional income to own your home "Free and clear" within five years is absolutely achievable to anyone ready to take the journey. Based on personal accomplishments and life experience, the steps laid out in my book work if you are ready to work them and stay the course. Please communicate with me! Let me know how I can help. The best way I can help you is to share my professional network and resources.

Your Life Journey and the Monopoly Board

You will need professional information and coaching. I am available. As you begin to "figure out" your ideal home, market conditions, home values and YOUR PURCHASING POWER, let me help you. I am here for you! Communicate with me via my website.

Can you really make more money and reinvent yourself? YES YOU CAN! And I can help you. There are hundreds of personal examples I can share with you that work! Just follow the simple steps I lay out in this book. You can accomplish all of this! You can "Own Your Home 'Free and clear' within five years." You can build a solid foundation for a thriving business that produces sustainable income, allowing you to purchase additional real estate and other investments to become fully, financially funded. Just imagine the life in front of you and all the new opportunities to pick and choose from.

Can you answer this question, "Will you have the optimal health to live a long healthy life to enjoy the results and new opportunities available to you because of your healthy finances?" You CAN have the healthy mind and body you've always dreamed of. What good is it to have all the wealth you've always dreamed of if you do not have the health to enjoy it? Follow the easy steps to Optimal Health. Take five minutes to communicate with Renee and me through www.HarvestWellness.com. At the site, you can purchase a copy of Dr. Andersen's Dr. A's Habits of Health and take the online comprehensive health assessment.

Closing Remarks

Owning your home "Free and clear" sooner than later is just the beginning of taking personal responsibility. It is the beginning of creating a mindset of independence and helping others to do the same. It's part of my "Big Why" I want to help people create Optimal Health, creating a healthy body and mind, so they can enjoy healthy finances, while encouraging others to do the same.

My big dream and hope is to see Southern California flourish with health, wealth and happiness, and for us to lead the rest of our great nation in the same direction. The government, politicians, media and Hollywood are not going to make it happen or even help. It's truly up to you and me to take advantage of the opportunities and resources within our reach to create an excellent life for ourselves and others.

It takes vision, courage, faith and discipline. It is not for everyone, but it is available to anyone who wants to take the journey. Join me and encourage others to come on the journey. Please keep in touch with me and let me know how I can help. May God bless and keep you along your journey.

Lloyd's Professional Network Resource
Here is a list of my immediate professional associates: Business and life coaches, attorneys, payroll services, insurance, medical doctors, financial advisors, general contractors, and many others are listed here.

Published in the book are only the names and professions. This is by design to keep all contact information current and relevant. For all current and updated contact information connect with them through my website www.SouthernCaliforniaRealEstateSystem.com.

The website is continually updated with new resources, professionals and opportunities. There you will find current real estate updates for Southern California, changes in laws and the tax code, health tips and relevant current events, just to name a few. You also have the opportunity to post your views, experiences, recommendations and tips.

Real Estate Consultation, Market Updates and Consultation

- California Association of Realtors®
- Bruce Norris, Real Estate Analyst; The Norris Group; Southern California Real Estate Trends and Updates
- Gene Wunderlich, Real Estate Analyst; Southern California Real Estate Trends and Updates
- Southwest Riverside Economic Development Corporation, Southern California Real Estate Trends and Economic Updates
- Lloyd Mize, Real Estate Broker and Business Coaching Consultant; Southern California, www.LloydMize.com or www.SouthernCaliforniaRealEstateSystem.com
- Dianne Hoffman, Commercial Real Estate Specialist; Southern California
- Todd Frahm, Attorney; Real Estate Law, Business Law, Estate Planning and Bankruptcy Specialist
- Aaron Lloyd; Sunset One Escrow, Escrow Services Real Estate, Business and Personal Property; Southern California
- Bill Provost, Lender/Mortgage Consultant; Southern California and Washington
- Tom Carter, Real Estate Title Insurance Specialist; Southern California

- Catherine Perrotta, DP Properties; Property Management Consultant; Southern California
- Tom Ferry, Your Coach; Professional Real Estate Coaching; National

Health, Wellness and Medical

- Dr. Wayne Anderson, author Dr A's Habits of Health, new book " Optimal Mindset, (thought process "How To Create Health") magazine, Success at Home
- Harvest Wellness Inc. (Renee Mize), Comprehensive Health System; www.HarvestWellness.com
- Dr. Jeremy Green, Chiropractor and Sports Medicine Specialist
- Dr. Alisha Moadab, Naturopathic Medicine Specialist
- Gina Reinecke, Health Coach
- Priscilla Montgomery, Professional Fitness Trainer, Body Builder and Coach; Southern California
- Bobby Kelly, author of "Body Solutions"; National Fitness Trainer
- Danielle Wohltman, Hair and Beauty Consultant

General Contracting, Development, Decorating and Design

- Deanna Marie, National Consultant; Interior Design and Restoration
- Keith Mathias, Broker and Contractor; Commercial and Industrial Development

- Coleen Wells; Wells Plumbing, Heating and Air Conditioning Service and Consultation
- Dale and Tracy Archer, General Contractor, Building and Remodeling Specialist; Southern California
- John McCabe; McCabe Nursery Landscape and Design General Contractor; Southern California
- Brent Longhurst; Pest and Bug Control Expert; Southern California

Life and Business Coaching/Transformational and Educational

- Jim McLaughlin, Professional Business Coaching; Transformational Coaching and Workshops; National
- Mark Nicole; Productive Learning and Leisure, Life Transformation Workshops and Coaching; Southern California
- Hal Elrod, Life Coach; Author of Taking Life Head On and The Miracle Morning; National Consultant
- Craig Duswalt, Rock Star Marketing; Entrepreneurial Master Mind Workshops; National
- Marcia Haygood, Educational and College Placement Consultant

Financial, Accounting and Insurance Services

- Monique Lambert, Pac Trust Bank; Personal and Commercial Banker; Southern California
- John Dubots; Dubots Financial Services; Financial Services, Income and Investment Advisory and Consultant; National

- Sean McHenry, Financial Advisor and Supplemental Insurance Consultant

- Jonathan Nolan, Health Insurance Consultant; Amante and Associates

- Jami McNees, Insurance Consultant; Commercial Workman's Compensation

   Tudd Frahm, Attorney; Real Estate Law, Business Law, Estate Planning and Bankruptcy Specialist

- Dule Dethel, Attorney; Estate Planning; Corporate Structure; Intellectual Properties

- Fred Karma and Nicole Albrecht, Financial Accounting Services; Corporate Structure, Income tax services

Business Professional Services

- Greg Preite, Online Profit Strategies; Business Website and Internet Placement Consultant

- Susan Goodsell, BNI Executive Director; Professional Networking

- Rick Ricards; Rick Ricards Marketing, Professional Outsource Marketing Strategies

- Mark Rowley, Payroll Services Consultant

- Victoria Rausch, Information Technology Consultant

- Peter Schlemmer, Owner; CEVA Productions, business marketing video production; Southern California

- Lynn Hawks, Owner; EXPERTS and AUTHORITIES, Business marketing TV productions; National

- Renee Mize, Mens Style Consultant, J. Hilburn Clothier, www.StyledByRenee.com

- Dawn Sneed, Owner; Olive Brand LLC, Executive Management and Business Services, www.theolivebrand.com

- Maryann Ehmann, Author, speaker, coach, "Breakthrough to Your Magnificent Life!"

- Maurice DiMino, Speaker, Author, trainer, creator of "Discover Your Million Dollar Message"

- Jonnie Fox, The Magnolia School of Etiquette and Protocol